How to Read Copy

Professionals' guide to delivering voice-overs
and broadcast commercials

Adrian Cronauer

Illustrations by
Tina Fornale

Bonus Books, Inc.

94 93 92 91 90   5 4 3 2 1

Library of Congress Catalog Card Number: 89-81891

International Standard Book Number: 0-929387-14-7

Bonus Books, Inc.
160 East Illinois Street
Chicago, Illinois 60611

Printed in the United States of America

Acknowledgments

From 1979 to 1986 I worked as a free-lance announcer in New York City. For a number of those years, I was also a part-time student and taught a course in voice-over techniques at the New School for Social Research. After I had been teaching for several years, the New School's Mary Carney Blake suggested I try to devise a way to teach my course through the mail, with students submitting assignments in writing and on tape. Her suggestion developed into a thesis project for my masters degree in media studies and that, in turn, developed into this book.

At the New School, Mary Blake was a constant and enthusiastic source of encouragement. So was Louis Giansante and, of course, Peter L. Haratonik, chairman of the Media Studies Department. I owe them all much gratitude. Tina Fornale, who provided the illustrations, is more than a good artist, she is a good friend. I also am grateful to the students who were my guinea pigs in developing these materials.

I received much help and encouragement from the people at Bonus Books. Initial encouragement about publication came from David Dietz, then manager of the Book Division at *Broadcasting Magazine.*

Most of all, I am indebted to my wife, Jeane, for her infinite forbearance while I constantly listened to student tapes and worked on the text. She put up with more noise and more inattention than anyone should ever have to tolerate. Moreover, she endured it with a smile.

Despite all the help I've received, I know there is still room for improvement in this work. Further, like any performing art, voice-over is an evolving craft with constant changes in style and approach. I flatter myself that there may be future editions and, with them, chances to correct mistakes and update whatever advice has become outmoded. That's where I hope to become indebted to you, the reader. If something bothers you, if you think something could be improved, if you know of a better way to approach a problem or are aware of a change in industry practices, please let me know. I wholeheartedly welcome any criticism, corrections or suggestions you may be kind enough to offer.

Adrian Cronauer
Arlington, VA
April 1990

Contents

Introduction

The well-dressed man with a graying beard says, "I'm Ed Bradley. Those stories and Andy Rooney tonight on 'Sixty Minutes'." The picture switches to a close-up of a stopwatch. As the second hand approaches the two-minute mark, the picture cuts to a shoulder-shot of a man's head. The man on the screen is silent, but a voice from somewhere off-camera says, "Ford consultant Jackie Stewart talks about the four cylinder turbo." The man on the screen begins speaking. When he finishes, the picture cuts to a shot of an automobile braking to a stop. The off-camera voice comes back to ask, "Have you driven the best built American cars? Have you driven a Ford lately?"

Both Ed Bradley and Jackie Stewart fall into the category of on-camera performers. But what about the unseen man who introduced Stewart and later gave the tag line? How is he described? The term for such a performer is *voice-over*, which describes quite well how the words are heard "over" a picture of something other than the speaker. The term refers, in one sense, to the finished product. Someone may tell you that he has just "done a voice-over" for such and such client. The technicians and production people, similarly, refer to that portion of the commercial as the voice-over. The term can also be used to indicate the person as well as the product of his work. Instead of saying "I do voice-overs" you could say "I'm a voice-over performer." Even shorter, "I'm a voice-over." During an appearance on "Late Night with David Letterman," Ernie Anderson described his job by saying, "I'm the voice-over for ABC prime time."

A purist may tell you that, technically, a voice-over is only a voice-over if it accompanies a picture—either live or on film or videotape. But in general usage, it is assumed that someone who does voice-overs not only narrates films and voices TV commercials, but does radio spots as well. There are two good reasons why this is so. When a commercial is part of an integrated campaign, the advertising agency will want the same voice on both the radio and TV versions. In addition, it takes identical skills, since in both cases, the speaker is not seen.

"Wait a minute," you say. "What skills are you talking about?" To answer that question would take an entire book—in fact, the book you're now holding. When you've finished reading this book you probably won't *have* all the skills needed to compete with professionals in the field; that takes months, even years of practice. But you'll *know* what those skills *are*, and when you do practice you'll know what you should be doing. More importantly, you'll know what you *shouldn't* be doing. That's vital. Practice alone won't accomplish much unless you know *what* to practice. Practicing the *wrong* things will certainly not lead to improvement. It will only serve to ingrain any bad habits you may already have. Study the principles outlined in this book, and you will have the foundation upon which to build your ability to take a piece of commercial copy, analyze it, wring as much meaning out of it as possible, and convey that meaning to a listener with naturalness, sincerity and believability.

"But," you may ask, "isn't that what all broadcasters do?" Well, yes. But only to a certain extent. The broadcasting industry is so specialized that each kind of performer uses different techniques to achieve his own particular result. Let's look at some examples of what a voice-over is *not*.

As we've already seen, there is an obvious difference between voice-overs and on-camera performers. When you're seen by the person to whom you're speaking, you have a wider spectrum of things to use other than your voice to get across your meaning: facial expressions, gestures and other body language. None of these are available to voice-overs. They must rely on *only* the voice.

News reporters and anchorpersons frequently are heard off-camera. But they are concerned with *communicating facts* as accurately as possible. So they use a far more formal approach and authoritative tone than is appropriate for most voice-overs.

Sportscasters are frequently drawn from the ranks of professional athletes. As such, they aren't expected to have the smooth, polished delivery of other broadcasters. They are chosen for their expertise in the sports field. Even if they weren't professional players, they are still expected to have a vast knowledge of all the major sports; how they are played, who the players are, and the history of the games and the players. Polished delivery is secondary.

Disc jockeys and other "personalities" aim to make you like them as persons. They exude cheerfulness and enthusiasm. They are, basically, entertainers; communicating information is a secondary concern at best and usually a means to better express their personality.

Good talk show hosts frequently spend more time listening than talking. When they do talk, they are concerned with putting guests at ease and drawing them out. To conduct a good interview, a host must remember that he represents the listener. He tries to ask the questions that the listener would ask if he could. He prepares thoroughly and rarely works from a prepared script. The host may have an outline or a list of possible questions to ask, but, beyond that, it's all ad-lib.

In fact, to one degree or another, all these categories of broadcasters need to develop their ad-lib talents. Not so, however, for voice-overs. In fact, any ad-libs are strictly frowned upon. A good voice-over will, however, make it *seem* as if he were ad-libbing. As we've seen, other kinds of performers need to impose their own personalities on their work. But with voice-overs, the *message* is all-important, not the speaker. Yet another difference: although the voice-over must understand what he is talking about, he needs no specialized knowledge. The voice-over doesn't need to prepare by reading books or articles or writing outlines and lists of questions. Still, as you will see, a specific type of preparation is needed. And in some ways, the preparation he does is far more rigorous than the preparation in any other type of broadcasting.

All of this, though, is not to say that voice-over performing bears no relationship to any other kind of performing. On the contrary, the skills and techniques outlined in this book are similar to those employed by stage and film actors, on-camera actors, and anyone else who must convey someone else's words from paper to a listener as though they were his own expressions. It is, essentially, an *acting* job.

You might have noticed that, throughout this introduction, I have used masculine pronouns in referring to voice-over performers. The reason is partly a matter of conventional rhetorical style and partly a reflection of the state of hiring practices in the industry. Traditionally, voice-over has been an almost totally male business. A possible explanation for this phenomenon is that, in the early days of radio, the equipment was unsophisticated and quite limited in frequency response. Early microphones had such poor reproduction quality that only a relatively small range of frequencies could be picked up. Consequently, deeper-toned voices were more easily understood. So early radio announcers were all male—and the more barrel-chested and bass the voice, the better. This mechanical consideration began the practice of using only male voices, and tradition kept it alive long after technical improvements in microphones and other audio equipment made such policies unnecessary. The conventional school of thought, which continued well into the sixties, was that a female voice could not carry enough authority. Since almost all producers were male, they had little incentive to question this unfounded assumption. But, with the rise of feminism, women began moving into jobs at advertising agencies other than the usual secretarial ones. As more and more commercials were produced by women, the old attitude began to change. Today, the majority of voice-overs are still being done by men. But for women, the field is a growth industry. Names like Tammy Grimes, Joyce Gordon, Cynthia Adler, Barbra Feldon, Sally Kellerman, and Fran Brill are as well known and respected in the industry as any of the top male voices. And the list is growing. So, also, is the variety of products that use women's voices for their spots. Granted, the majority of products using female voices falls into categories like women's clothing, cosmetics, and household products. But the times do seem to be changing. Joyce Gordon, for example, has done spots for ABC Sports and General Motors. And her GM spot was concerned with the technical design of an energy-absorbing suspension, not the traditional "feminine" aspect of interior design!

Although voice-over is indeed a growth industry for women, that isn't to say it is an easy field to break into, for either men or women. Some say the only field more competitive than voice-overs is high-fashion modeling. The reason for all the competition is that if you are successful, the money is very good. First, you get paid for the original recording session. If there is more than one version of the spot, you get paid for each. For some categories of spots, you get more money every time the spot airs. After a certain period (usually thirteen weeks) you get paid again. And that continues for each thirteen-week cycle as long as the spot is on the air. Even when it goes off the air, the agency may want to keep open their option of pulling the old spot out of their files and using it again in the future. So, to make sure you don't start doing commercials for one of their competitors, they pay you what is called a "holding fee." Every cycle! For every spot they may want to use again!

On-camera performers also make good money. But with on-camera work there's always the problem of overexposure. After you've appeared on-camera in several spots, someone is sure to say, "Let's not use him again. His face is getting to be too well known." It's an understandable reaction; people generally remember faces much more readily than voices. So, regardless of how many voice-overs you do, there will always be more work for you.

Since the field is so lucrative, it is also highly competitive. To become one of the relative handful of people who do most of the work you have to devote a lot of time and effort to marketing yourself. In the latter part of this book I'll suggest some techniques for self-marketing. But no matter how much you market yourself as a voice-over performer, you won't succeed unless you are better than the competition. There are specific skills you can learn, and this book will introduce you to these skills. After that, it takes practice—lots and lots of practice.

The part of this book devoted to producing a demo reel contains a section entitled "Where does the copy come from?" It suggests sources for commercial scripts or copy you can use on your demo reel. These same sources can be a rich source of practice copy as well. At the end of this book you will find a collection of sample copy. Some of it can be used for practice, but most of it is designed to be used with assignments you will find in various parts of the book.

Should you be working on your own rather than as part of an announcing class, you might want to find at least one other person who can work along with you. Critique each other. Letting someone else evaluate your work can be a great help by exposing you to another viewpoint. You'll learn quickly how a single piece of copy can be interpreted in a variety of legitimate ways. You'll also discover some mistakes you never would have realized you were making without input from someone else. Moreover, by correcting another person's work, you will become adept at objectively applying the lessons you are learning to your own work.

In addition to the practice assignments, you will be instructed, from time to time, to do some "experiments." These fall into two categories: "head" experiments, and "action" experiments. The head experiments are not meant to really be done. You can, of course, actually carry out most of them if you choose, but you can do them just as well in your mind's eye. Visualize yourself going through the instructions and picture the results. The action experiments, on the other hand, should be done precisely as the instructions indicate. Both kinds of experiments are designed to illustrate specific points, so whether you're doing a head experiment or an action one, don't simply follow the instructions. Think about what you've done and what you have learned from it.

You'll also find instructions at various places in the text directing you to listen to recorded examples on the enclosed audio tape. Each cut on the tape supplements the written information covered in the text by demonstrating specific voice-over principles and approaches. When you are directed to listen to a specific tape cut, stop reading! Listen to that cut before you read any further. Don't put off listening to it. These materials have been field-tested to determine the precise place to incorporate taped components for *optimal* results.

For the same reason, don't listen to any cut before you have read the appropriate material in the book. Each cut relates to a specific part of the text, and you will get the most value out of the combined package if you refrain from listening to any part of the tape until you have read the section designed to prepare you for that particular example. In other words, don't listen to any part of the tape until you have been instructed to do so by the text. When you *are* instructed to listen to a tape cut, don't read any more until you have heard the cut.

There is no single correct way to read a given piece of commercial copy. Each voice-over person will have a different way to approach the same spot. But there are a lot of universal rules that they all will follow. This book will tell you what these rules are. Rules, of course, should be viewed as guides to intelligent action, not as straitjackets. But the first step is to learn the rules thoroughly. Only when you have mastered the rules will you have enough skill and sophistication to effectively decide when it is more effective to break one of them.

"I wasn't interrupting...I was doing a voice-over."

Tools of the Trade

1—Microphone Technique

Presence

Let's begin with a head experiment. Picture in your mind a large room. Choose a room you are familiar with; it might be a banquet hall at a nearby hotel or the gymnasium at a local school. Imagine you are with a friend in that large room. Picture your friend standing as far away from you as he possibly can. You, meanwhile, are seated comfortably, with your eyes tightly closed. Your friend speaks to you, perhaps reciting a poem or reading a newspaper article. Imagine your friend, as he is speaking, walking toward you. At some point, he stops and, still facing you and still talking, he walks backward. Then he stops again and stands completely still but continues to talk.

With your eyes closed, you cannot see where your friend is standing in the room. Nonetheless, you are able to pinpoint where he is from moment to moment—solely from the sound of his voice. If you are like most people, you won't have the slightest trouble knowing exactly where your friend is. How can you tell? To what clues is your brain responding?

There are three vocal qualities that combine to tell you how close a speaker is. The first, and most obvious, is volume. The closer the source of a sound is to your ear, the louder it seems to be. However, when we're listening to the human voice, volume alone isn't a very accurate indicator of distance between speaker and listener, because of an interesting psychological phenomenon. If your friend had started speaking while standing across a large room from you, he would have instinctively spoken in a loud voice. He might even have yelled at you. But as he came closer, without even thinking about it, he lowered his volume. Had he continued walking toward you until his mouth was only an inch or so from your ear, he would have unconsciously dropped his voice to just above a whisper. What he did, of course, made perfect sense. If, while walking toward you, he had continued to use the same high volume with which he started, you would, at the very least, have thought him to be rather rude. So we see the actual volume isn't too valid an indicator of distance between speaker and listener.

But something else happened that gave you a better clue to the distance of the speaker. Raising or lowering the volume of your voice also changes the *quality* of your voice. The amount and the nature of the harmonics, or overtones, changes.

There's also a change in *pitch.* Most people, when projecting their voice over what they perceive as a distance, have a tendency to raise the pitch, or tone, of their voice in addition to raising the volume. If we were listening to a singer, we would say she moved to a higher key. A general rule you will observe is: the louder the voice, the higher the pitch. This change in both the pitch and the harmonics of a voice gives our brains important clues about a change in the distance between ourselves and the speaker.

The third clue we use in determining the nearness of a

sound source has to do with how sound travels, physically, to our ears. The only thing we are consciously aware of hearing is *direct* sound, sound that travels in a straight line from the source to our ears. However, almost all the sounds we hear are really a mixture of direct sound and *echoes*. Of course, we are only aware of echoes when they bounce off an object at such a distance—a canyon wall, for example—that it takes a full second or so for the reflected sound to reach us. Yet, even though we may not be aware of it, almost everything we hear has an echo. Sounds bounce off floors, ceilings, walls, furniture—almost any surface will reflect sound to some degree. Usually, the reflecting surfaces are so close to us that the echoes take only a tiny fraction of a second to reach us. We are unaware of them, but the part of the brain that processes sound is fully aware of the echoes. The number of echoes and their relative strength compared with the original, direct sound provide information which the brain processes much like an analog computer. The higher the ratio of reflected sound, the farther away the source seems to be. Conversely, a high proportion of direct sound and relatively little reflected sound makes the source seem very close. This quality of sounding close to the listener is referred to as *presence*.

LISTEN TO CUT I ON THE INSTRUCTIONAL TAPE.

Microphone Placement

Watch rock singers on TV. Their lips are literally touching the microphone. Johnny Carson, on the other hand, uses a desk mike that's at least a foot away from his mouth. During his monologue, his voice is picked up by a boom-mike three or four feet above his head. Why the difference? Which of the three is the proper way to position a mike? Well, they all are, really. Microphones have different characteristics and are designed to be used in different environments, so the way they should be used differs as well.

With the average microphone designed for recording the voice at normal speaking volume, the proper distance be-

tween mike and mouth is approximately eight inches. This is
sometimes referred to as "the rule of thumb" because that distance can easily be approximated by making a fist with the thumb
and little finger extended. This distance is close enough to provide a relatively high amount of direct sound with correspond-
ingly little reflected sound and, therefore, good presence, but
isn't so close that it causes saturation (a problem we'll get to
shortly).

Projection

The next time you have a chance to watch someone talk on the
telephone, pay attention to the volume of their voice when they
are talking to you as compared with when they are speaking on
the phone. Frequently, you'll find their telephone voice is much
louder than their normal speaking voice. It's as though they feel
compelled to overcome the distance they perceive between themselves and their listeners by shouting across the miles. In the

early days of long-distance service, equipment was primitive and people frequently did have to shout to be heard on the phone. Children observed their parents increasing their volume when speaking on the phone and imitated them. Their children imitated them. Phone service, meanwhile, kept improving, but nobody seemed to notice. Unaware of what they were doing, they kept right on shouting on the phone and their children kept right on imitating them. To this day, many people still shout on the phone and are completely unaware that they are doing so. These same people, when faced with a microphone, revert to their telephone behavior. Since they can't see their listener, they automatically overproject.

Another group with a similar problem is professional actors. Many have had it drummed into them that they must be heard distinctly by members of the audience in the most remote row of the highest balcony. The habit has become so ingrained that whenever they are required to perform, they automatically begin to project by raising the volume of their voice, even though it may be totally unnecessary.

Still others overproject because they, either consciously or not, feel they must "sound like an announcer." Unfortunately, they have a mistaken impression of what an announcer should sound like. Television sitcoms have contributed greatly to this mistaken impression. The man on the street thinks an announcer should have a style somewhere between Jim, the anchorman on "Murphy Brown" and Ted Baxter on the old "Mary Tyler Moore Show" with touches of Dr. Johnny Fever from "WKRP in Cincinnati."

Still, sitcom characters usually reflect people's impressions rather than create them. So where did this bizarre idea of announcing come from? Like telephone-shouting, it has roots in what was once a technical necessity. In the very early days of radio, live orchestras were used to provide the theme music which accompanied the opening and closing announcements of shows. Most studio orchestras were at least eight to ten members strong; for elaborate network shows, bands of thirty or forty or more instruments were not unknown. Against such an avalanche of sound, the poor announcer was forced to literally shout just to hear himself over the din. Incidentally, that's why the old-time radio announcers would cup one hand over their earlobe—the gesture burlesqued by Gary Owens on "Laugh-In." The hand over their ear actually helped them hear themselves better. These early announcers developed distinctive styles which, invariably, included massive amounts of overprojection. New announcers would emulate the style of the old pros and the stereotype became fixed.

With the advent of television came game shows. Announcers like Don Pardo in New York and Gene Woods or the late Johnny Olsen in Los Angeles found they had to be heard above a wildly cheering studio audience. In self-defense, Pardo, Woods, and their clones shouted. Shouting became their style. Folks at home, meanwhile, assumed that to be an announcer you had to talk, at the very least, quite loudly.

Of course, you don't have to do anything of the kind. On the contrary, to sound natural and believable, you have to use only the same small amount of projection you use in normal conversation—perhaps even less.

You can determine the proper voice level quite easily by performing another experiment. This is an action experiment, so you'll need a friend to help you. Tell your friend to look straight ahead. You face her from the side. As you tell your friend a joke, a story, or relate some incident that happened to you, gradually move closer to her until, using the rule of thumb, you reach a point about eight inches from her ear. You will have instinctively lowered your voice. Note how softly you are now speaking. That is precisely the volume you should use when speaking into a microphone; no more! You'd never dream of shouting into your friend's ear. Since the microphone represents your listener's ear, you can't shout into it, either. What you should aim for is a normal conversational tone.

Working the Mike

Although the standard amount of projection is the same as what you would use in normal person-to-person conversation, there will be occasions when it will be necessary to project less or more.

Let's say, for example, that the copy begins with the line:

I've just discovered an important secret!

If you were really sharing a secret with someone, you wouldn't shout it from the mountaintops. You'd become conspiratorial. You'd drop your voice almost to a whisper so that no one could possibly overhear you. That's what you have to do when you encounter this kind of copy. The same approach is appropriate when you want to sound mysterious, romantic, or seductive. Deliver the copy at a volume even softer than your already relatively low conversational level.

When you drop that extra level, you have to get closer to the mike to obtain the right amount of presence and overcome competition from extraneous noise.

Conversely, some copy demands an overabundance of enthusiasm.

**Wow! My Toyota dealer just made me a deal
you wouldn't believe!**

Even if the sense of the material didn't tip you off, the first word, "Wow!" almost demands that the line be delivered with substantial energy. To properly deliver such copy, which is usually referred to as "hard sell" or "punch" copy, it's necessary to project more and use more volume. In such a case, it's also necessary to back away from the mike.

This business of moving closer to or farther from the mike is referred to as *working the mike*. The rule is quite simple. We've already talked about how the microphone should be approached the same way you would approach your listener's ear; the closer you get, the softer you talk. Working the mike is just another way of applying the same principle: the softer you speak, the closer you need to be to the microphone, while the louder you are, the farther away you need to be.

There's one other way of working a mike that you should know about. But, before discussing it, let's first talk about how microphones are constructed. There are thousands of microphones on the market. They range in price from a few dollars to thousands of dollars. And yet, they are all similar in that they all are designed to respond to the mechanical vibrations in a given medium—almost always sound waves in air—and convert the kinetic energy of those vibrations into corresponding electrical energy. The most common way to accomplish this is by allowing the incoming sound to strike a lightweight movable diaphragm. The vibrations of the diaphragm are converted into a very weak electrical current which matches, almost point-for-point, the original sound waves. This electrical current is amplified and otherwise processed to produce, in the loudspeaker, a representation of the sounds which originally hit the microphone.

Being mechanical devices, microphones have a limited range of volume over which they operate properly. If a sound is too soft, the diaphragm won't move enough to generate a usable current and the sound will be drowned out by the ambient hiss, hum and crackle that inevitably sneaks into audio circuits— what's generally called *noise*. This is, incidentally, another reason why you need to work the mike more closely when you speak at an unusually low volume; probably a more important reason than the need for added presence.

If the sound is too loud, it can create even worse problems. It can literally overload the microphone. The diaphragm moves as far as it physically can and, even though the air pressure from sound vibrations may be pushing it farther, there isn't any more room for it to move. So it stops. The system reaches its limit and, for an instant, stops operating altogether. In that instant, what occurs is sometimes called a "pop." This instantaneous overload, known as saturation, most frequently happens when the speaker utters a consonant sound which requires her to expel a substantial amount of air. The most common offenders are what speech therapists sometimes refer to as *plosives, stops* or *stop-plosives.* The plosives are p, t, k, b, d and g. Other consonants occasionally cause the same problem, but the single most common cause of microphone saturation is the "p" sound. Hence, you will frequently hear this phenomenon referred to as "popping your p's." Avoiding such saturation is another reason why you must work farther from the mike when doing copy requiring a lot of energy and enthusiasm which makes you instinctively raise your volume.

In addition to increasing the distance between mouth and mike, there is a second way to avoid popping your p's and, in most cases, it's the best remedy of all: work the mike *off-axis.*

When you talk directly in front of the mike, and the mike is pointing directly at your mouth, you are said to be *on-axis.* When you work on-axis, the puffs of air created when you utter the offending consonants come out of your lips and go directly into the microphone. As an action experiment, hold your hand about two inches away from your mouth with the palm facing you. Now, say the word "popcorn." Notice how you can actually feel the puffs of air from the initial "p," and the "k" sound in "corn." Now, as you continuously repeat the word, rotate your hand slowly to a position facing your cheek. You'll discover that you only have to move your hand an inch or two to lose the feeling of the puffs of air. Try the experiment again, only this time move your hand up toward your eyes and down toward your chin. Again, you'll see that you don't have to move your hand very far to escape the direct puff of air. What you have been doing is, simply, moving your hand from an on-axis to an off-axis position. You can do the same thing with a microphone.

Aside from instances when it is necessary to prevent saturation, microphones should almost always be worked directly on-axis. Sometimes, an inexperienced person will think he's on-axis when he isn't. This happens because it looks as though the

ONE WAY TO WORK A MIKE OFF-AXIS

mike is pointing straight at him. But instead of pointing the mike at his mouth, what he's done without realizing it is to point it at his eyes. Be wary of this tendency, and take care that the mike always points directly at your mouth.

Because the diaphragms in many of the more expensive microphones are sensitive and delicate, they can easily be damaged. Almost everyone has, at one time or another, seen someone walk up to a public address mike and blow into it to see if it's working. Although they don't need to be supersensitive or to have superb frequency response, P.A. mikes do need to be sturdy and to withstand a lot of rough treatment. They are deliberately designed in a way that trades off sensitivity and response for durability. They can withstand plenty of abusive treatment, such as people blowing into them. With delicate studio microphones, however, such treatment can permanently damage the diaphragm or other internal structures. So make it an ironclad rule never to blow into any mike. The best way to test a microphone is simply to speak into it. If, for some reason, you aren't able to test it by speaking, try gently tapping the external casing with your fingernail. But never, never, never, under any circumstances, blow directly into a microphone. If you do, you may find yourself paying for an expensive but useless piece of electronic equipment.

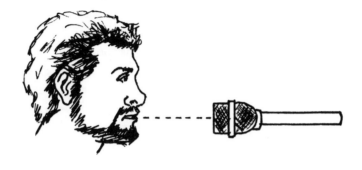

THIS

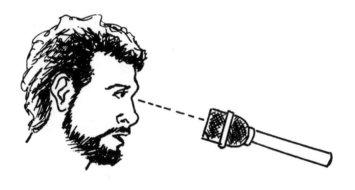

NOT THIS

Posture

Speech is accomplished by exhaling air from the lungs in such a
way that the vocal chords are forced to vibrate at an audible frequency. If you can't breathe, you can't speak. If your breathing is
inadequate, your speech will, likewise, be inadequate.

The most important organ involved in breathing, next to

the lungs, is the diaphragm. In contrast to the small, delicate dia-phragm in a microphone, the human diaphragm is a large, fairly sturdy muscular wall located beneath the pleural, or chest cavity. Breathing occurs when muscular effort enlarges the chest cavity. The diaphragm moves downward, creating a vacuum, so air rushes into the lungs. When the diaphragm moves back up, the chest cavity contracts, forcing air out of the lungs. Muscles of the back and those attached directly to the ribs can expand the chest cavity a small amount and, alone, can enable a person to take small, shallow breaths. But really deep breathing can only be ac-complished through movement of the diaphragm.

A person sitting in a chair, leaning forward, shoulders hunched, is physically incapable of much diaphragmatic move-ment. Such a posture forces the diaphragm up and keeps it there. But someone standing erect with a straight back and head held high can comfortably take in large quantities of air. Prove it to yourself. Try this action experiment. Stand tall and completely fill your lungs with air. Holding your breath, sit down and lean for-ward, resting your arms against your knees, a table, or a desk. Hunch your shoulders. You'll feel quite uncomfortable until you let your breath out. Then, so long as you hold the same cramped posture, you will be unable to take a full, deep breath. Since there's no place for your diaphragm to go, you can only breathe by expanding your ribs, which results in only small, shallow breaths.

Most recording studios, to make it easier for performers to breathe diaphragmatically, are set up so that the performer stands. The copy is placed on a podium or music stand, and the mike is attached to a boom which extends above eye level. Should you encounter one of those rare studios where the microphone is on a table-mount and you have no choice but to sit while speak-ing, remember the need for full diaphragmatic breathing and make a deliberate effort to sit as straight and erect as possible. Likewise, when practicing with a tape recorder at home, work in a standing position so you will develop good breathing habits.

II – Recording Studios

Like any generic term, the words "recording studio" can be used to describe a wide array of facilities, ranging from tiny, one-person announce booths to large halls capable of accommodating full symphony orchestras. Technical capabilities of a given recording studio may be as limited as a single microphone and a single, monophonic tape recorder. Or, they may be able to mix hundreds of audio sources onto dozens of channels while adding a lot of sophisticated electronic effects.

But physically small or large, technically simple or complex, all recording studios share certain similarities. They all have at least one microphone to pick up sound and convert it to a fluctuating electrical signal. There will always be an amplifier to boost the weak signal to a usable strength. And, of course, there must be a device that will make a lasting impression of that signal on some recording medium, which usually means a tape recorder. Speakers are needed to monitor the sound being recorded and, afterward, to listen to the resulting recording.

Soundproofing

With speakers blaring, machines clicking and whirring and people talking, recording studios can be pretty noisy places. None of this noise, however, belongs on the recording being made. So all recording studios have some way of acoustically isolating the area in which the microphones are placed. In fact, the word "studio" is frequently used to designate the separate area where the performers perform, and the rest of the recording complex is called the control room or the control area.

Elaborate measures are employed to prevent unwanted noise from ruining the recording; not just sounds from the control room, but from outside, as well. Unwanted sounds can easily intrude when someone slams a door down the hall or walks heavily across the floor above. Traffic outside, subways underground, and planes overhead can all ruin an otherwise perfect recording. To prevent such intrusions, thick, sound-absorbing insulation is packed into the wall and ceiling spaces; "floating" false floors are constructed and solid double doors are built with air spaces between.

Still, keeping out unwanted sound is only part of the process of soundproofing. Acoustical engineers, when planning a recording studio, spend a lot of time and effort to ensure that recordings made in that studio will have as much presence as possible. As we've already seen, presence is a function of the ratio of direct to reflected sound. It follows, then, that studios are carefully designed to have as little reverberation as possible. The technical term used by engineers is *anechoic* which means, literally, free from echoes. Various devices are used to achieve an anechoic environment. Walls are deliberately set at angles that avoid parallel surfaces. Floors are thickly carpeted. Walls and ceilings are covered with acoustic tiles or other sound-absorbing material.

The result of all this careful planning is striking. People who have never experienced an anechoic environment find it takes a bit of getting used to. Although we aren't consciously aware of room reverberation when we speak, we do hear it, and when it suddenly is gone, it startles us. A student once described it as feeling as though her words didn't go anywhere. "They just seemed to come out of my mouth, fall on the floor and lie there," she said. Another student, who suffered from acute claustrophobia, felt as though he couldn't breathe inside the studio. Most people don't react so severely, but it is a new and unsettling experience.

Strange as it may seem to suddenly be deprived of any room reverberation, an even more startling experience, for someone used to working only with an inexpensive home recorder, is to hear oneself played back in full fidelity on professional equipment. The contrast is like the difference between a snapshot taken with a tiny disc camera and a color portrait taken and enlarged by a professional studio photographer.

There are things you can do to lessen these reactions to working in an unfamiliar environment. First, use the best quality equipment you can afford for your practice at home. If you aren't using this text in conjunction with a formal class that provides you with access to a professional studio, you can still visit a professional studio on your own. Book a small amount of time to make a recording of yourself reading some practice copy. Listen to it. Do it again. Then listen to that cut. Keep it up for the full period you have booked. (Most studios book time in multiples of one hour. Some, however, will be willing to charge on a half hour or quarter hour basis. See the section on Making the Reel in Chapter 8.) You should gain this professional studio experience fairly soon. It is important that, from early on, you be aware of the limitations of your inexpensive home machine.

Studio Protocol

When you show up at a recording studio for an audition or an actual job, it will be assumed you are a professional. As such, you will be expected to do certain things and to know enough not to do other things. A complete list of everything you should and shouldn't do under every circumstance would be arbitrary and endless, but there are a few items that are considered standard operating procedure throughout the industry.

The first thing you need to consider when you enter the studio is where to stand. Sometimes, you'll encounter nothing more than a microphone on a floor stand. Simply position yourself about eight inches from the mike. Remember the rule of thumb? Of course, you won't actually hold up your fist with your thumb and little pinky sticking out. By now, though, you should have practiced enough at home that you can pretty well estimate the proper distance by just looking at the mike. You'll have to

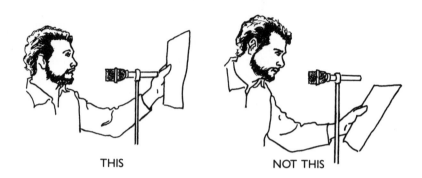

THIS   NOT THIS

hold your copy up at eye level. Don't hold it so low that you need
to lower your head.

If there is a copy stand, put the copy on it and take a
stance so that you can comfortably read the copy. Don't be afraid
to adjust the stand if it isn't at the proper height for you. They expect you to be comfortable.

Don't ever, however, even *touch* the microphone—or the
mike stand—much less adjust it. The only person who should
touch the mike is the engineer. There are two very good reasons
for never touching the mike. One is practical, the other political.

Practically, you can't possibly know as much about that
particular mike as the engineer does. As was pointed out a while
back, there are thousands of different microphones on the market. Each has its own particular characteristics. In fact, a professional quality mike usually comes with a little booklet describing,
in arcane technical language, how to set the mike up and adjust it
for optimum response in a variety of circumstances. They even
have little diagrams showing the mikes' response pattern and how
it varies when the mike is adjusted in different ways. The engineer, whose job is to make you sound as good as possible, has
read this booklet. You haven't. If you sincerely want to sound as
good as possible, let the engineer worry about the mike.

Even if, by some quirk of fate, you happen to be an expert on that particular model of microphone, the rule still holds: don't touch that mike! Why? Simply because it isn't your job and, especially in highly unionized studios, you can get yourself into serious political trouble by doing something that falls within the scope of someone else's job description.

Level Checks

Before you start recording, the engineer needs to set the volume. She may also want to reposition the microphone and make other technical adjustments. To do so, she needs an audio source, so she will ask you for a *level check*. Or she may just say something like "let's try it once for a level."

What she's asking you to do is to read the copy—and this is very important—*exactly* as you intend to do it when she starts to record. In other words, for a level check, you *must* deliver the spot just as though it were an actual *take*. This point is emphasized because there is a natural tendency to hold back a little when we know the tape recorder isn't running. We unconsciously try to save ourselves for the real thing. All too often, a performer will give a halfhearted level check. Then, when he starts to do the first take he gives it all he has. The volume increases by thirty percent, the meters are jammed at the top of the scale, the recording is ruined and the engineer has to readjust her settings while she calls the performer an unflattering name under her breath. She probably won't say anything, she'll just let him continue and she'll use the first take as a new level check. When he finishes she may say something about technical problems or may, without any explanation at all, just ask for another take. The performer, without realizing it, has just marked himself as inexperienced and less than professional. Everyone in the control room knows what happened and will remember it the next time that performer is considered for a job.

There are two other things to remember about level checks. First, keep going until the engineer tells you to stop. Usually, you'll only have to read four or five lines. If, however, you reach the end of the copy and haven't been told to stop, go back to the top and read it again. And again, if necessary. You might feel a little silly, but it's necessary, so keep reading until you're told to stop. Besides, the extra practice will do you good. Second, when you're asked for a level check don't ever, under any circumstances, say "Hello, testing. . .one, two three. . .testing." Nothing will more quickly and certainly mark you as a rank amateur.

Slates

After the recorder is running but before the spot begins, a few words are said to identify the recording. This identifier is called a *slate* and, in actual recording sessions, is almost always done by the engineer or producer from the control room. At auditions, however, the talent (that's you) is frequently required to do the slate. If you aren't sure, ask, "Are you going to slate it or do you want me to do it?"

If you have to do a slate, what do you say? The answer depends on what information will be needed when they listen to that recording. If it's an audition, all they need is your name and the cut number. They already know the product name; every cut on that reel of tape is a different version of the same spot for the same product. The only variable is the particular speaker and, if there is more than one attempt by a single individual, a number, so they can tell one cut from another. "John Doe, cut one." "John Doe, cut two."

At an actual recording session, different information is needed. Although, in practice, the engineer almost always does the slate, there will be rare instances when you will be asked to do it, and you should know what information to provide. To begin with, they don't want your name. You're the only person there so there's no need to differentiate your version of the spot from someone else's. That same studio, though, may have recorded a dozen other commercials for as many different products on that same day and it would be disastrous if a spot for Pepsi were to get mixed up with one for Coke. So the product name, though never identified in the slate for an audition, is the very first item mentioned at an actual recording session.

It's not unusual to do two or more spots for the same product at a single recording session and there has to be some way to tell, without listening to them, which spot is which. Even if you're only doing one spot that day, that same studio has probably done other spots for the same product. Advertising agencies assign numbers to their spots and each slate, in addition to the product name, should include the agency's spot number. Occasionally, there will be more than one version of the same spot; one, a full minute long and the other, only a half minute. You have to identify which one you're doing. And, of course, the cut number. "Savarin Decaffeinated, number SCS-257, thirty second version, take one."

As a point of interest, the term "slate" derives from the motion picture industry where each spot is preceded by a picture of a written identifier. An assistant cameraman holds up a device consisting of a blackboard on which the necessary production information has been written with chalk. Above the slate portion is a hinged piece of wood that can be slammed against the top edge of the blackboard frame, producing a sharp sound similar to a very loud hand clap. This device, therefore, is called either a "clapboard," or a slate.

Once the camera is rolling, the assistant director might say, "All right, let's have the slate" or, simply, "Slate it." Whereupon, the assistant cameraman holds the clapboard before the camera while reading aloud the information written on it. He then slaps down the hinged piece of wood. The resulting sharp crack on the audio track is later lined up with the film frame in which the hinged piece of wood first makes contact with the edge of the clapboard. Picture and sound are thus perfectly synchronized. Over time, the term "slate" came to refer not only to the

clapboard, but also to the words spoken by the production assistant. The word eventually became so generic that a slate now means anything, visual or oral, used to identify a recorded performance.

A Steady Stance

Once the engineer has her level set, you are expected to be consistent. Nervousness, though, makes a person fidgety. One of the things people do when they are fidgety is to sway back and forth, which of course changes the mouth-to-mike distance. This results in a fluctuation of levels; you sound as though you're fading in

PROPER STANCE

and out. To avoid this problem, plant your feet firmly about two feet apart and rest your weight evenly on both feet.

Unwanted Sounds

A lot of effort has been expended by acoustical engineers and designers to insure that no unwanted sounds will intrude on recordings made in their studios. Such effort, however, can be futile if the talent, himself, introduces extraneous noises during the recording session.

The most common way a performer can create unwanted sounds is by moving paper. If you have a copy stand, put the script on it and, while the tape is rolling, never touch the copy. If you don't have a stand, firmly grasp the copy a little below the middle of the page and hold it at about eye level. Don't wiggle it, don't rattle it, don't move it at all. If you have two pages, put them side by side on the copy stand. If you don't have a stand, hold the first page in your left hand directly in front of you. As you approach the end of the first page, slowly and silently move the second page, in your right hand, to a position directly below the first one. Your eye can make a smooth transition to the next page, and you can slowly and quietly remove the first page to the side. Keep it in your hand, though. If you let it drop when you finish with it, the paper will hit the floor, making a noise.

Other sources of unwanted sound include bracelets and necklaces as well as other jewelry and heavily starched shirts and blouses. In fact, any kind of fabric that rustles when you move should be avoided when recording. Wear only soft, unstarched fabrics. Take off the jangly jewelry.

The Bitter End

When you finish a take, if you're pleased with what you've done, you'll feel a great sense of relief. You'll want to sigh or to physically slump or step back from the mike. If you're dissatisfied, there's a temptation to express your dissatisfaction, sometimes in graphically scatological terms (look it up). In either case, fight that urge. Most audio engineers will tell you they would love to have a dollar for every time they've seen an otherwise perfect take ruined by paper rattles, foot shuffles or some other sound overlapping the last syllable of the last word. Once the last word has escaped your lips, freeze! Don't utter a sound; don't move a muscle. Don't even breathe. Stand there as still as a statue while, in your mind, you count "one thousand one, one thousand two." After that, you can scream, shout and carry on to your heart's content.

The Most Important Tool—Your Voice

Oh, wad some power the giftie gie us
To see oursels as others see us

. . . Robert Burns, 1786

I—How You Sound—to Yourself and to Others

Self-Image

Nobody really likes the sound of his or her own voice on tape. This is as true a statement as you will ever read. Even professional announcers, who have for years been hearing recordings of themselves, still don't like their voices. They usually get to the point where they can tolerate and even accept how they sound. But they never really *like* it. The reason for this involves a concept called *self-image.*

Each person carries in his mind an idea of what he thinks he is like: how he looks, how he acts and how he sounds.

This self-image is less than totally accurate because it is formed from incomplete data. The way you believe you look, for example, is determined by what you see each day as you comb your hair, shave or apply makeup. What you see in a mirror, though, is necessarily a direct, head-on view. Without some elaborate arrangement of multiple reflecting surfaces such as a tailor's mirror, it is impossible to ever see yourself in profile. So your idea of what you look like is always a head-on view, never a profile.

Now, think back to the first time you saw your profile in a home movie or video tape. Your reaction, certainly, was one of shock. You probably thought "That can't really be me! It doesn't look a bit like me." Of course, it did look like you; it just didn't look like what you *thought* you looked like. The clash between what you were seeing and your self-image caused your less than delighted reaction.

Something similar happens with your voice. What you hear as you speak is not what others are hearing. You, and everyone else, hear your voice as it travels through the air. But you alone also hear it as it resonates through your jaw bone, your nasal cavities and other parts of your head. The result is that what you hear as you speak is deeper and more resonant than what others hear. Still, it's what you've become used to and what you've incorporated into your self-image. When you hear yourself on tape, your inevitable reaction is "That can't be me! It sounds so high-pitched, so whiny. It sounds like a little kid!" Your voice doesn't really sound child-like to others; only in comparison with your overly resonant self-image. Were you to hear a tape made so long ago that you no longer remembered making it, and did not realize you were listening to yourself, you probably would consider your voice quite pleasant to listen to. This fact is born out by a number of professional announcers who have reported similar experiences. As one announcer described it, he was casually listening to his car radio when he heard a commercial he had recorded several years earlier. At first, he listened with only marginal attention, yet felt the voice he was hearing was easy to listen to and handled the copy professionally. Then, when he realized he was listening to himself, his whole attitude changed. He became critical and less at ease, less content in his listening experience.

Your Normal Tone

When you begin listening to your own voice on tape, the tendency is to compensate for the discrepancy between your self-image and what you hear on the recording by lowering your voice. Your intention is to sound mellow and professional. The result, alas, is to sound phony and amateurish. To really sound your best, you need to speak in your normal voice. As an action experiment, try this test. To insure that you are using your normal tone of voice, say out loud "Uh-huh" as though you were answering a question. Say it again. Now say "Uh-huh, one." Again. Now say "Uh-huh, one, two, three." The tone in which you said the last phrase is your *normal tone*—the tone in which you should read all copy.

Once you have found your normal tone, practice it until you use it habitually while reading copy aloud and don't have to think about it anymore. At that point, you can forget about sounding mellow and devote all your attention to conveying the meaning of your copy to your listener.

II—Style: What to Do with the Voice You Have

The Curse of the Small-Station Lilt

As already mentioned, many people have a false idea of what an announcer should sound like. This conception of an announcer-like sound includes, in addition to over-projection, a pattern of inflection* frequently referred to as a *small-station lilt.* It's called that because it's almost always found at small radio stations but rarely, if ever, at large ones.

Newcomers to the broadcasting industry traditionally begin their careers at low-power stations in small markets where they gain experience and hone their skills. It's good training in a wide variety of broadcasting skills because one man does it all; disc jockey, newscaster, engineer, and weatherman. But, with so much going on, there isn't any time to study copy, analyze it, explore different interpretations, and practice. In fact, the first time an announcer at a small station sees a piece of copy, frequently, is when she reads it on the air.

As a matter of necessity, small-station announcers develop a lilting inflection pattern allowing them to give a serviceable reading to any piece of copy even if they've never seen it before—what's called a "cold reading." By their very nature, cold readings are usually passable, but never very good because the all-purpose inflections used bear little relationship to the content of the copy and, therefore, convey little meaning.

LISTEN TO CUT **2** ON THE INSTRUCTIONAL TAPE.

The meaningless inflection pattern of the small-station lilt is what many people mean when they talk about someone "sounding like an announcer." Actually, though, that's the last thing a good announcer wants to sound like. The proper goal of an announcer is to sound as though he's *not* announcing at all, but merely having a one-way chat with a friend. If you try to sound like an announcer, you are heading in precisely the wrong direction.

---

* Only a portion of the meaning of spoken language is carried by the words. Much of the meaning of what we say comes from the *way* we say it—the inflections we use. A simple phrase, "Is that so?" can convey surprise, curiosity, interest, skepticism, disbelief, sarcasm, or hostility depending on the inflection used.

Dialects

At a party in Virginia, a visiting New Yorker complimented his hostess on her delightful southern accent. The lady gave him a puzzled look. "What do you mean?" she asked. "I don't have an accent. It's you Yankees who have the funny accent." She was absolutely right, of course. Regional dialects are relative. By definition, everyone speaks with some kind of dialect. It's only when yours is different from everyone else's that it becomes noticeable. The speech of the New Yorker stood out in Virginia, but back in Manhattan, where everyone else spoke the same way, he sounded perfectly normal.

An announcer, regardless of his regional dialect, is perfectly acceptable if all his listeners speak with the same dialect. A problem crops up, though, when an announcer is heard all over the country. If he has a southern drawl it, will be noticeable to northern listeners. Someone with a New England accent, like Cliff Clavin on "Cheers" or the Pepperidge Farm cookie man, will only sound normal to listeners in New England.

A noticeable dialect is undesirable because it calls attention to itself and distracts the listener's attention from the message being delivered. The only regional dialect that does not call attention to itself is the one spoken in midwestern America: an area usually regarded as starting in western Pennsylvania and covering Ohio, Michigan, Illinois, Indiana, and a few other states west of these. There are some variations in the dialects spoken in this area, but for the most part, they all sound pretty much the same. This midwestern-American dialect is the standard for the broadcasting industry in this country. If you have a midwestern dialect or can develop one, your chances of success in broadcasting and, particularly, in voice-overs, is tremendously improved.

Still, a dialect other than midwestern doesn't mean that you have no chance at all. An actor named Eddie Barth, who speaks with a pronounced Brooklyn dialect, has done thousands of commercials. He specializes in a working-class tough-guy sound. Barth has been so successful that among many advertising agency casting departments, someone who sounds like an uncultured roughneck is said to have the "Eddie Barth" sound.

Pseudo-Conversational Style

Earlier, it was mentioned that the goal of a good announcer is to sound as though he is merely having a one-way chat with a friend. Such a style is sometimes referred to as *conversational*. Strictly speaking, though, the word "conversational" isn't accurate in describing what we're after.

You will find below a transcription of a conversation among three people. You'll immediately notice there is neither punctuation nor capitalization in this transcript. Keeping in mind that the speakers are all intelligent, literate, well-informed, and accustomed to speaking in public, please read through the transcript and write in the proper punctuation and capitalization according to the standard rules of English grammar. Remove any stammers, repetitions or hesitations by crossing through them.

Transcript of a Portion of "This Week with David Brinkley"

uh the uh two members of uh the senate gramm and rudman have become at least as famous as abott and costello

dont forget hollings

for much the same reasons

and hollings uh he is usually left out i guess for reasons of brevity and saving space in the headlines but in any case the three of them composed a bill that said how they believed the bu the federal budget should be balanced in five years this week a district federal district court knocked out a section of it so is it dead sam what

yeah its dead if the supreme court reaffirms it and congress doesnt pass another law to try to correct the constitutional problem because the section they knocked out was the automatic trigger section which says if you don't come up with a thirty six billion dollar a year reduction in the deficit each year until its zero then there will be automatic across the board no holds barred budget cuts well the supreme court or the the lower courts said by giving that power to the comptroller general you were giving it to someone who did not constitutionally have it now i think what will happen is that the congress may correct it but if they dont then gramm rudman is dead george

yes but the president

are you ready for the gramm rudman the bills funeral

well i would i would preside and, unh throw the first handfull of dirt on the casket i think its a lousy bill but i think the bill is alive and well its easy to correct congress created a guillotine they appointed an executioner the court said you have to get another executioner cause that guys uh not removable by the president its easy to do and they have to do it because they have wrapped themselves as the president did in his state of the union address he wrapped himself in gramm rudman as in the flag it is now a national icon and they simply cannot allow it to die because of some little perfecting amendment that theyd be reluctant to pass

but thats to miss an irony because for congress to come back and and suggest perhaps that all right so make the comptroller general somebody who can be fired by the executive branch is an is in in essence to say the same thing that the president has been saying all along give me line item veto power give me the final word which they will steadfastly continue to do which is why ironically in the end theyre going to be forced to be to kill off gramm rudman i will throw the flowers as you throw the dirt and they will have to do what they were elected to do and what they are paid to do which is make decisions about cuts in the budget and then vote on it

george they have wrapped themselves in a shroud and i think they would be well done in disposing of it and let the courts do it

well thats

hunh the courts cut the budget

thats thats a very poor simile to wind up on here but im sorry time is up thank you all

——— When you have finished punctuating the transcript, **LISTEN TO CUT 3 ON THE INSTRUCTIONAL TAPE** with your eyes closed. Note how smoothly and understandably the conversation flows. Finally, play the same cut again while comparing it to the corrected transcript.

The preceding exercise was designed to demonstrate a number of things about casual conversation. First, the way we punctuate writing isn't always appropriate for the spoken word. Media expert Tony Schwartz has correctly observed that we could not communicate effectively if we spoke the way we write. We'll come back to this point in Chapter 7 when we talk about marking copy.

The second thing you should have noticed about the conversation you punctuated was that it did not run smoothly. Like almost all extemporaneous speech, it contained hesitations, stutters, and stammers. The speakers stopped in midsentence to start a new sentence. There were numerous um's, uh's and er's. All of these imperfections are part of normal conversational speech. Our goal is to develop a style that avoids these imperfections while still retaining the naturalness, believability, and informality of tone of casual conversation. To emphasize this distinction, we say that we are striving to achieve a *pseudo-conversational* style.

A third lesson illustrated by this exercise is how little of the meaning of material is carried by the words alone, and how much by the voice—the pauses, the choice of inflection, and the energy level.

II – Qualities to Strive for

Believability

Despite all the imperfections inherent in genuine conversational speech, it does have one important characteristic: it is believable. You know the speaker isn't just mouthing someone else's words. Something tells you the ideas are his own just as the words are his own. His words carry meaning because he emphasizes all the right words in exactly the right way. The inflections he uses are perfectly suited to the content of what he says. The speed of delivery and his tone of voice are just right, the pauses come where they should and only where they should. Yet he never has to give a conscious thought to such technical matters; it all happens automatically as the speaker concerns himself with the *meaning* of what he's trying to say. So long as you start with a thought and try to express that thought, you'll never have a problem sounding natural and believable. It's only when you reverse the process, when you start with words instead of ideas, that you sound unnatural and unbelievable.

To make someone else's words sound really believable takes a lot of careful work. The skills required aren't developed without a lot of practice. But the qualities of naturalness and believability are the ultimate goal all good announcers strive to reach; the *sine qua non* of the announcer's art.

Non-Intrusiveness

In the early days of television, most of the people working in the new medium were veterans of radio. They, naturally enough, approached television as though it were simply radio accompanied by pictures. Many early commercials, therefore, consisted of nothing more than an announcer holding up a product and talking about it. Some of these relatively primitive commercials were, nevertheless, quite effective in increasing sales of the sponsor's product. But only *some* of them; others produced no results at all. Why the difference? Extensive research finally revealed that a distracting picture element in the unsuccessful commercials—perhaps an unusual pattern in the announcer's necktie—was drawing the viewer's attention away from what the announcer was saying. Such distracting picture elements came to be known as *vampire video* because, like the legendary vampire, they bled strength, in this case from the selling message.

The solution to vampire video was simple once it was understood: get the announcer out of the picture and show only the product, turning the on-camera announcer into a voice-over. Today, commercials are carefully pre-tested to make sure they don't contain any vampire video.

It is quite possible for a commercial to also contain audio elements which are distracting—what we might call "vampire audio." Improper use of music and sound effects can, obviously, interfere with instead of enhance the intended effect of a commercial. The announcer himself can be a source of vampire audio. Any part of an announcer's style that calls attention to itself should be avoided. Expressing one's own personality is fine for sportscasters and disc jockeys, but in commercials, the message is the important thing—always the message.

Summary

If we look back over this chapter, we can see that all we've discussed can be boiled down into a single sentence: always strive to be believable, natural and non-intrusive.

Commercials and public service announcements are designed to persuade listeners to act in a particular way. "Buy this!" we say. "Use this gasoline or detergent or toothpaste!" "Give to the March of Dimes!" "Vote for Smith for Congress!" "Support public television." In most cases, we give the listener a reason to do what we urge. We extol product attributes. We play on feelings of pride, greed, patriotism, guilt or any of a whole panoply of other emotions. We promise the advantages to be gained by doing what we suggest. Yet all our wheedling and cajoling will be for naught if the listener doesn't believe us. No amount of persuasion, no elaborate promises, no earnest pleas will convince a listener to so much as move her little finger if she doesn't believe you.

People generally dislike being shouted at, lectured to, or preached over. Sure, when the material in the copy makes it necessary, it is not only appropriate but also required of you to sound excited and enthusiastic. It's only natural to sound hyped-up when you are trying to impart exciting news. The key is to sound *natural*. Excessive or unwarranted enthusiasm causes people to become suspicious. Their natural skepticism kicks in and they begin to wonder what you're really up to. "Where," they ask themselves, "have you hidden the fourteen-karat bamboozle?"

Before you can get people to believe you, you have to get them to pay attention to what you are saying. And they won't be paying attention to your message if they're thinking about something else. You have to get rid of as many distractions as you can, and that includes anything about your delivery that calls attention to itself rather than to what you are saying. You should avoid anything in your performance that might constitute vampire audio.

The Printed Word

When I use a word . . . it means just what I choose
it to mean—neither more nor less.

. . . Humpty Dumpty in
Alice's Adventures in Wonderland
by Lewis Carroll

I–Copy Analysis

If it were possible to telepathically transmit a pure idea from one mind to another, it would be an example of perfect communication. Occasionally, one hears rumors about secret Pentagon projects involving telepathic communication, but, unfortunately, few if any people are sufficiently adept at transmitting and receiving telepathic signals to make this mode of communication very reliable. Hence, we are forced to rely on words as a medium to convey ideas. Words, however, introduce what communications theorists refer to as *noise*. By noise they mean anything that interferes with the perfect transmission of a message.

With words, the element of noise arises from their imprecise nature. Take, for instance, the word "chair." It doesn't conjure up a very precise image. Ask a group of people to draw a chair and see how different their ideas of a chair really are. We can make it more precise, of course. "A black leather Danish modern reclining chair with a circular base made from chrome-plated tubular steel with a matching footstool." Now we have a much clearer picture; what the communications theorists would refer to as a more precise semantic referent. But it's still not perfect. Is the body of the chair covered with finished leather or suede? Is it upholstered and cushioned? If so, how thickly? Are there arms? Are they upholstered? How high is the back? One could go on for an entire paragraph or even a whole page and still not have given enough information to conjure up a totally precise picture of the chair in every minute detail.

We can be grateful that in everyday discourse we can apply some common sense, and only need to supply as much detail as we think necessary to get across an approximate idea of what we are talking about.

Semanticists classify words according to their level of abstraction. Fairly common words, like "chair" have a fairly low abstraction level. Their meaning can be relatively precise. By the time you reach the seventh level, however, there can be substantial confusion about a word's exact meaning. If you were to go out on the street and ask the first ten people you meet to define "love" or "peace" or "justice" you would get ten different definitions. Granted, there would be similarities. But there would also be substantial disagreement as to the details. Obviously, then, words are imprecise vehicles for conveying meaning.

Because of their imprecision, words introduce noise into the communications process. The speaker starts with an idea and tries to find those words he believes will most accurately express that idea. But his vocabulary may not contain a word with the precise meaning he wants. So he has to be satisfied with a word that only comes close, although he may modify that word with others in an effort to better express his intended meaning. Already, though, some noise has been introduced into the process; the original idea has lost a little bit of its meaning.

When the words reach the listener, she must search her vocabulary for their meanings. It's possible she doesn't know a specific word at all—in which case she must infer, from the context, what she imagines the speaker meant. More likely, the listener will recognize a word but her concept of what it means will differ from what the speaker intended to convey. More noise; more loss of meaning!

When it comes to reading commercial copy, another serious source of noise enters the picture. Speakers in face-to-face situations use gestures and facial expressions to help convey meaning. Even when the listener can't see the speaker, there are still important clues to meaning carried by the tone of voice and the inflection used. The voice-over person picking up a piece of commercial copy has none of these aids to comprehension. Here, the idea originated in the mind of a copywriter. She is the one who decided which words would be chosen to express her idea and then committed those words to paper. All the announcer has to go by are words printed in black and white—no facial expressions, no tone of voice—nothing but words on paper. From these and these alone, before he can do anything with the copy, he must divine the copywriter's original intent. Admittedly, there is an element of guesswork involved, but there are techniques which, if carefully and methodically employed, will ensure that any guesses made are well-educated ones, any choices, the most probable ones.

II–The Four Basic Questions

As soon as you begin to work on a piece of copy—before you do anything else—decide on answers to four questions. Your answers should not, of course, be random guesses. Rather, they should be dictated by the copy itself; the style in which it's written, the choice of words, the rhetorical devices used and the level of vocabulary. Your answers to these questions will, more than anything else, determine the overall approach you will apply to the copy.

Question Number One: To Whom Are You Speaking?

Think about your favorite radio station. Where were you when you last listened to that station? In the bathroom taking a shower? In the kitchen cooking a meal? Driving your car? Now try to recall who was there with you. Next, think of your favorite television program. Again, remember when you last watched that show. Who, if anyone, was there with you. In both cases, chances are you were either alone or in the company of only one other person. It's almost always true. Listening to the radio and watching television are largely solitary activities. Furthermore, a listener or viewer has no way of knowing if anyone else, anywhere, is tuned to that same station. If she were asked about it, she would say she assumes there must be a lot of other people tuned to that station. After all, broadcasters couldn't stay in business without an audience. But she has no direct physical evidence of anyone else sharing the program with her. She doesn't know who they are, where they are or exactly how many there are. Most important of all, she doesn't care. They aren't there with her. She isn't aware of their presence. There is no group dynamic, which, incidentally, is why they have to put laugh-tracks on comedy programs. Her relationship is direct and personal—one-to-one—between herself, the listener, and you, the speaker.

Here is a truth you can carve in granite: THERE IS NO SUCH THING AS THAT GREAT BIG AUDIENCE OUT THERE IN RADIO OR TELEVISION LAND. We hear about it, but it is a myth. It *does not exist!*

One of the first radio personalities to realize this was the late Arthur Godfrey. At his peak in the 1950s he was, after President Eisenhower, perhaps the best-loved man in America. The secret of his success, as reported in a *Time* article, came to him as he lay abed after a near-fatal automobile accident in 1931. He should not, he realized, announce to listeners, but, rather, should talk to them, one on one. "There is no radio audience, just one guy or one girl in a room," he said. "If the audience is 'ladies and gentlemen' together, they have better things to do than hear me on the radio."

Never, therefore, think of speaking to a group because *there is no group!* In broadcasting, one always speaks to a single person. Always think in the second person singular (you, my friend). You can be certain you're heading for trouble if you catch yourself thinking in the second person plural (folks, friends, you-all, you guys). Unfortunately, there are some copywriters who simply don't know what they are doing. You will occasionally encounter their work—a piece of poorly written copy containing phrases such as "all of you listening to me now." Here you have no real choice. You're stuck with the copy as written; you don't have the option of changing it. In such cases, remember that it's all right to say it, but don't think it. Keep your mind-set in the singular.

The knowledge that you are speaking to a single individual leads to one of the most useful techniques an announcer can use: mentally picturing your listener. One of the reasons it's so difficult to read copy naturally and believably is that we're talking to an inanimate object—a microphone. Talking to inanimate objects is an activity we rarely engage in. In fact, those who habitually talk to trees or refrigerators are usually considered to be in need of professional counseling. Talking to a microphone seems unnatural. It feels unnatural. Is it any wonder that it comes out sounding unnatural?

There are some situations when a person may *seem* to talk to inanimate objects. A good example is the cab driver who shouts maledictions at another car. The car is merely a symbol for its driver. The cabbie isn't actually calling the other car nasty names, he's really cussing-out the other driver. Similarly, you must understand that the microphone is only a symbol of the listener and, by mentally picturing the listener, you make it much easier to sound natural and believable.

Probably the easiest way to picture your listener is to think of someone you know; your spouse, a cousin, a neighbor, or a co-worker. Of course, the person you choose to speak to has to fit the copy. It wouldn't make much sense to talk to a young, devil-may-care bachelor about baby care products. You wouldn't talk to a ten-year-old girl about easy mortgage loans and it's doubtful your great-grandmother would be seriously interested in a high-performance motorcycle. The copy content must dictate what *kind* of person you will be speaking to.

Your answer to the first question must lead you to mentally picture *a specific person*. It won't be any help to you if you cop-out on this question by saying something like "a parent." A parent can come in any of a variety of shapes, colors, sizes, temperaments, economic levels, cultural and ethnic backgrounds and may be either of two possible sexes. It's impossible to produce a picture of a prototypical parent because no such animal exists. Instead, you have to come up with a particular parent; a specific person you can visualize.

Similarly, an answer to the first question such as "a person who wants to save money" isn't any help to you since nobody knows what a person who likes to save money looks like. It might be George C. Scott made up to look like Ebenezer Scrooge. Then again, it might just as well be your Uncle Milton who insists on wearing those atrocious ties he buys at the local flea market. No matter, this answer doesn't help create a *specific* person.

A more elaborate cop-out on this question is to rephrase copy points or product attributes into personal traits. It doesn't help you much to answer this question with something like: "an active young man who likes the taste of cola drinks but, because he's trying to keep fit, he's afraid of what additional calories will do to his waistline. He also doesn't want the kind of chemically-induced high he gets from caffeine." This kind of analysis doesn't help you visualize the listener. All it does is go through the copy, point by point, and state that your nebulous person is someone who is receptive to those particular copy points.

Keep it in the singular. An answer such as "a family" or, even "a husband and wife" comes close in that it is possible to visualize a specific young couple. Still, in normal conversation, you wouldn't talk to both of them at once—not unless you're capable of looking at one with your left eye and the other with your right. What you actually do when talking to a couple is shift your gaze and your attention back and forth from one to the other. In face-to-face situations, you can only speak to one person at a time. So, when analyzing a piece of copy, choose a single person to visualize and speak directly to only that person. (Remember Arthur Godfrey's comment?)

There will come a day, though, when you're confronted with a piece of copy for a product with such a narrow appeal that you won't be able to think of a single person you know who would be a potential purchaser of such a product. Suppose you're handed a commercial for luxury condominium apartments in Manhattan where purchase prices start at five hundred thousand dollars for an efficiency on a lower floor, and go all the way up to six million for the penthouse. Few of us know anyone with that kind of money. In such a case, you have to imagine someone who does fit the category: a wealthy stockbroker, perhaps, or a Park Avenue plastic surgeon. But you can't stop with only a vague job description. Spend some time thinking about it. Construct, in your imagination, a whole person. How tall is he? What does he weigh? What color is his hair and eyes? How old is he? Is he married? To whom? Do they have children? How many and how old? Does he like sports? Which ones? Does he play or just watch? What other hobbies does he have? What kind of car does he drive? Where did he go to school, undergraduate and graduate? What was his major? How much money does he make? What's his net worth? Think of any other details that will help you to actually visualize your imaginary person and how he acts. The more detailed you get, the better.

Visualization is the important thing here. You must be able to see, in your mind's eye, the person to whom you are speaking, because it will affect the *way* you speak. We speak differently to a mail carrier than we do to a police officer. We speak differently to a college professor than we do to a grade school student. We speak differently to our lawyer than we do to our auto mechanic. And we speak differently to our parents than we speak to our children. To the former, you might politely suggest, "Dad, I'm really not sure it's such a good idea for you to do that, don't you think?" With the latter, you're more apt to adopt a commanding tone: "Son, stop that! Now!" This example points out the necessity of the second of the four basic questions.

Question Number Two: What Is Your Relationship to the Listener?

If you choose an actual person to visualize as your listener, your relationship with that person already exists. If, however, your listener is imaginary, you'll have to imagine your relationship as well. In the example of the Park Avenue plastic surgeon, you may be a patient, an old college roommate or, perhaps, a friend he plays golf with on weekends. Maybe you are his tax accountant. A golfing companion telling him how a wonderful new golf ball will improve his drive would use an entirely different approach than would his accountant discussing a promising real estate investment. Who you are in relation to your listener will greatly influence the way you talk to this imaginary person. The choice you make, of course, will be dictated by the content of the copy.

Question Number Three: What Is Your Relationship to the Product?

Unless you already use the product and are thoroughly delighted with it, you will probably have to imagine your relationship to the product, as well. Suppose you drop in on a neighboring homemaker for a mid-morning cup of coffee and the conversation turns to cake mixes. You tell her about a new Duncan Hines mix. How do you know about it? You could be a homemaker who happened to try it and got good results. Or you might be a former home economics major who is now the neighborhood authority on gourmet cooking. It is never sufficient to say only that you are a company spokesperson. By virtue of the fact that you are doing the spot, you are *ipso facto* a company spokesperson. The important question remains: what *kind* of a company spokesperson? An automotive test driver will talk about motor oil differently than a mechanic. Both would approach the subject differently than a petroleum engineer. Your choice, of course, would again be dictated by the copy itself. If it talks about how well this new oil makes the car perform, the best choice of the three would probably be the test driver. Your approach, then, would be enthusiastic with, perhaps, a touch of both boyishness and machismo. If, however, the main point of the copy is that this oil makes your engine run smoother and last longer with fewer breakdowns, it's more likely to be the mechanic talking, so your style would be more friendly and folksy. If the copy goes on about the oil's viscosity, additives and detergency level, it's a fairly safe bet that you're speaking as the petroleum engineer. As such, you'll want to sound authoritative, professional and intelligent—maybe even intellectual.

Question Number Four: What Is the Motivator?

This question, depending on the particular piece of copy, could be paraphrased two ways: What emotion are you appealing to? Or, what need are you promising to fulfill? Sometimes you'll get the right answer either way. If, for example, a spot appeals to the emotion of anger, it is probably offering to assuage the need to achieve or dominate. An appeal to insecurity will promise to alleviate the need to feel safe. In an article published in the communications journal *Et Cetera*, Jim Fowels of the University of Houston lists fifteen basic needs that advertising can appeal to. It is interesting to note that, as one might expect, the need for sex leads the list. But, surprisingly, physiological needs come in last on the list.

1. The need for sex
2. The need for affiliation
3. The need to nurture
4. The need for guidance
5. The need to aggress
6. The need to achieve
7. The need to dominate
8. The need for prominence
9. The need for attention

10. The need for autonomy
11. The need to escape
12. The need to feel safe
13. The need for aesthetic sensations
14. The need to satisfy curiosity
15. Physiological needs: food, drink, and sleep

These fifteen needs aren't the only ones, just the most frequently encountered. As you work with different pieces of copy for a variety of products, you'll discover many more powerful needs and emotions that can be used to convince a listener to think or act in a particular way.

Discovering the underlying motivation is the most important clue of all as to how to approach a piece of copy. If you're trying to scare your listener, you'll want to use a sinister tone of voice. If you're trying to seduce your listener, you'll want to sound very soft and intimate. Whatever effect you want to have on your listener should directly affect the way you approach the copy.

A piece of copy that tells how Kodak film helps you to preserve cherished memories, keeping them fresh and alive through the years, would hardly be read with a fast, breezy, up-beat style and a high energy level. On the other hand, a line like "Dodge trucks are ram-tough!" would sound a little ridiculous delivered in a soft, wimpy tone of voice. Always be sure that the style of delivery is in keeping with the image and the nature of the product itself.

So the first step in analyzing any piece of copy is to decide on the best possible answers to the four basic question: 1) To whom are you speaking? 2) What is your relationship to the listener? 3) What is your relationship to the product? 4) What is the motivator? Unless the answers to all four questions are clear in your mind, it will be impossible to do an optimum job of delivering the copy believably, naturally, and non-intrusively.

III – Common Copy Formats

There are many ways to write a commercial. But a few formats have proven so successful they have become standard throughout the advertising business. Because they occur so frequently, you should be familiar with them. Train yourself to recognize the particular format being used and know how to deal with each one.

Problem—Product—Solution

Probably the most common of all copy formats starts by setting up a problem. The sponsor's product is then introduced. Finally, it is alleged or, sometimes, demonstrated that the product solves the problem. Everyone has seen a spot with a woman in what is presumed to be a neighborhood laundromat. There's a laundry basket in front of her. She's looking into the basket with a pained expression when another woman enters the picture. The newcomer is evidently a friend because she knows the first woman's name. "What's the matter, Jane?" she asks. "Oh, it's this dingy laundry," Jane replies as she holds up a towel, "I just can't get it really clean." There! The problem has been set up. Jane has been cursed by dingy towels. But her friend knows what to do. The friend holds up a box of the sponsor's detergent. "Here," she says, "try new All Temperature Cheer." Now that the product has been introduced, either Jane's friend, or the voice-over will probably elaborate on how Cheer is able to get even the dirtiest laundry clean and bright. At the end, we'll see Jane again. Only this time, her original worried expression has been replaced by a beaming smile. She's holding up a towel and says, either to the camera or to her friend, "Just look how white and bright! New All Temperature Cheer really did the job!"

A recent television spot uses absolutely no audio at all, and yet is a quintessential example of this copy format. An innocuous-looking man holds up a piece of cloth—perhaps his own tie—which he soils with ketchup, grease or some other hard-to-remove stain. He places several ice cubes in a cocktail shaker, along with some water and a small amount of All Temperature Cheer. Then he puts the soiled cloth in the shaker and shakes it for a short while. He opens the shaker, removes the cloth and proudly shows how miraculously clean it has become.

Turn now to the sample scripts section in the back of this text and see which of those spots you can identify as falling into this category.

The spots you should have identified as examples of the problem-product-solution copy format are: Merrill Lynch, Samsonite, and Bank of New York.

When confronted with this problem-product-solution type of spot, there are three distinct feelings for you to convey in sequence: When you present the problem, you should sound worried or, at least, concerned. When you introduce the product, you should sound proud and hopeful. Then, when the results are in, you should be happy, even delighted, with what the product has accomplished.

Introduction—Elaboration—Summary

This commercial format follows the same formula that has been used for decades to write everything from magazine articles to term papers to after dinner speeches. It's simply: 1) Tell them what you're going to tell them, 2) tell it to them, and 3) tell them what you've told them.

For an example of this kind of copy, turn to the sample scripts section in the back of this text and read the Gimbels spot.

Note that the entire message of the spot is contained in the first two lines of the copy. Gimbels is having a sale in which Hoover vacuum cleaners have been marked down anywhere from

15 to 50 percent. Next, we encounter just over five lines which drive the point home with specific details. The last sentence re-states, in capsule form, the spot's message: "So save 15 to 50 percent now during Gimbels' biggest Hoover sale ever!"

As in the problem-product-solution type of spot, there are three distinct parts of the spot requiring three different ap-proaches. But instead of sounding concerned, proud, and happy, this kind of spot needs one emotion throughout—happy or excited—but at differing intensities. To understand why we ap-proach this kind of copy in this way, think about what happens in actual face-to-face conversation. Let's imagine that you meet a good friend on the street. She comes over to you and asks with substantial energy, "Are you still looking for a good vacuum cleaner?" When you nod, she continues, "Well, I just went to Gimbels and they're having a sale on vacuums!" You happen to be near a park bench, so you both sit while she elaborates, "I just got one for myself. Look." She opens a shopping bag to show off her new purchase while she tells you about the good price she got. She's still happy and excited, but she's become more matter-of-fact as she gets into the specific details. Next, she pulls from her pocket a newspaper ad she has clipped. Pointing to the ad, she suggests several models of cleaners you might want to con-sider and shows you how much you can save during the sale. While discussing various models, her level of enthusiasm drops further, but when she gets to the savings, her enthusiasm climbs a little. As she stands to leave, her energy level also rises until she is near the level of excitement she showed when she first met you and told you about the sale.

The example above is typical of the way we engage in normal conversation. Even though we may be very happy and ex-cited over a new discovery that we want to share, when we start to describe the nuts-and-bolts details of how it works, we have to be-come less excited, more matter-of-fact. This natural flow from a high to medium energy level and then back up again gives us a model to follow when we encounter the "introduction-elaboration-summary" copy format.

You have, of course, already pictured in your mind the person to whom you are talking. Now imagine yourself rushing up to that person with some exciting news. Once you have his attention, you go into the details explaining, perhaps, how tab "A" is inserted into slot "B." Your excitement is tempered. Once you've explained it all, though, you expect your friend to become equally excited, so to encourage him, your energy picks back up to the original level for your big finish. That's precisely the approach to use whenever you encounter the introduction-elaboration-summary copy style: high energy and enthusiasm at first, moderate energy in the middle, and renewed energy for the final summary.

Product Comparison

A third common copy format uses a comparison—either between the sponsor's product and the competition, or between those who use the product and those who don't. Sometimes, the copy simply states the facts of the comparison and leaves it up to the listener to draw the obvious conclusion.

Please turn to the sample scripts section in the back of the text and read the Fiat spot.

All the Fiat spot really says is that Fiat's competitors all suffered sales slumps last year while Fiat had its best year ever. That's it! The listener is left to infer that there must be something inherently good about Fiat and bad about the competition to account for these facts. The key to reading comparison copy effectively is to be sure there is a difference between the way you talk about the competition and the way you talk about the sponsor's product. As noted earlier, you want to speak about your product with pride, while theirs, depending on the characteristics of the particular copy, might be spoken of with a variety of subtle tones: sorrow, pity, disdain, or, as in the case of the Fiat spot, even a tone of bemused condescension. The most important word in the last sentence is "subtle." Your aim should be to convey an under-stated nuance; subliminal, rather than blatant.

Now turn to the back and read the spot for Pilot Life.

Instead of comparing the sponsor's product with the competition, this commercial compares the relative disadvantage of those who do not avail themselves of the sponsor's product with the superior position of those who do. Since the listener you're trying to reach is someone who doesn't yet use our prod-uct, we don't want to alienate him by speaking of him in an unflat-tering tone. We don't, therefore, sneer or condescend to him, so we might try friendliness and understanding with a bit of con-cern. The client, of course, is still spoken of with pride and posi-tiveness.

Mood Pieces

Some commercials make no attempt at any sort of argument, logi-cal or otherwise, as to why someone should buy the product. In-stead, the entire spot is an attempt to establish in the viewer's mind a connection between the product and a particular mood, attitude or feeling. An excellent example of a mood piece would be any of the series of commercials that have been running for the past several years on "Saturday Night Live" for Budweiser beer. They use modern graphics and high-tech special effects to convey the idea that Budweiser is a modern, with-it, youth-oriented product. Similarly, the series of television spots for Sun-kist Orange Drink don't even mention good taste, low calories, caffeine-free, or any of the other standard selling points for soft drinks. Instead, to a jingle taken from the Beach Boy's old hit "Good Vibrations," we see healthy, tanned young people, usually blond and frequently in bikinis, playing in the surf, tossing a beach ball and obviously enjoying themselves to the fullest. The implication is that Sunkist, somehow, is connected to being young, healthy and attractive. Almost all mood pieces are made for television—probably because pictures are so evocative of moods. Many use only music for the sound track. But some mood pieces also use voice-overs. For an example of such a spot, turn to the copy in the back of the book for Home Pride.

This spot, like any good commercial, has only one aim and it pursues that aim relentlessly: to bring to the viewer's mind a sense-memory, the taste of butter, and to associate that sense-memory with the product. Note that the sponsor's product isn't even mentioned until almost halfway through the spot.

In the case of this Home Pride bread commercial, the mood is enjoyment of the taste of butter, so you should adopt the mood of a gourmet describing his favorite dish. You should strive to make your listener hungry—even to make him salivate. It might even add to your performance if you were to do the spot on an empty stomach so you can salivate a little yourself.

In analyzing this kind of copy, your answer to the fourth question, "what is the motivator?" is directly related to the mood the sponsors are trying to create. If you are lucky enough to be able to see a playback of the video for the spot, you will find it a big help in answering this question. More likely, you will only have a script. Frequently, the script will have a video column like this spot for Precisely Right Home Permanents:

VIDEO	AUDIO
OPEN ON WOMAN IN WIDE BRIMMED HAT, HER HAIR IS COVERED. SHE SPEAKS WITH CONVICTION.	WOMAN (OC): I'll *never* perm my hair again.
SHE REMOVES HAT, BEAUTIFULLY PERMED HAIR TUMBLES OUT.	That's what I said, until I discovered
SHE HOLDS UP PACKAGE	Ogilvie's Precisely Right. The perm that promises—
ON CUE, SHE UNDERSCORES WORDS "PRECISELY RIGHT" ON PACKAGE.	in writing—your next perm will come out Precisely Right.

VIDEO	AUDIO
CUT TO WAVING LOTION BEING PREPARED. SUBTLE LIGHT THROBS BEHIND BOTTLE TO DENOTE HEAT.	It works with this exclusive self-heating formula.
DISS TO WOMAN (FLASHBACK) IN PERMING PROCESS FEELING THE PLEASANT SENSATION OF HEAT.	As the heat cools, the waving process automatically slows down.
CUT TO WOMAN IN PRESENT, SHOWING OFF HER LIVELY BEAUTIFUL CURLS.	So, no over-processing. You get beautiful, long-lasting curls—everytime.
CUT TO ECU PKG; REPRISE UNDERSCORING OF "PRECISELY RIGHT."	Get the perm that promises—in writing
WIDEN OUT OF ENTIRE PACKAGE.	—your next perm will come out Precisely Right.

With just a little imagination, you can use the video column to visualize the pictures that will accompany your words. If you are able to see a storyboard, it can be an even greater help in understanding the mood of the spot. Storyboards are drawings or photographs of key scenes from the commercial's video with the corresponding audio printed below each frame. An example of a storyboard is on the next page.

We have examined some of the more common copy formats: problem-product-solution, introduction-elaboration-summary, product comparisons, and mood pieces. Although you will encounter copy that doesn't fall neatly into any of these categories, they are common enough that you will encounter them

FCB

Kleenex Softique.

"Runny Nose"/Non-New :30
KKKS 5033

1. (MUSICAL FANFARE)
ANNCR (VO): Kleenex® Softique®
introduces "The Runny Nose".

2. (SFX: CRASH)
NOSE: Achoo!

3. ANNCR (VO): No wonder
runny noses get sore.

4. NOSE: Ooh! Aah!

5. ANNCR (VO): Many tissues are
really irritating.

6. NOSE: Ow! Ow! Ow!

7. ANNCR (VO): That's why
sensitive noses run into...

8. (SFX: BONK)
...Kleenex® Softique® tissues.

9. NOSE: Achoo! Achoo!

10. ANNCR (VO): Unlike ordinary
tissues, Softique® has special softness
fibers fluffed up for the softest touch
ever from a Kleenex® tissue.

11. NOSE: Ahhhhhh...

12. ANNCR (VO): Softique®.
For softness that's right on the nose.

again and again, and should be thoroughly familiar with the ways
to handle them.

IV – The Copy Closing

Once you have answered the four basic questions and have determined the copy format, there is one final thing you should look
for in your analysis of a piece of commercial copy: the closing.
The final sentence or two of any commercial is vitally important,
since it is the last thing the listener hears and, therefore, leaves
the strongest impression in his mind. Regardless of the copy
style, there are two things to look for in final sentences: the "call
to action" and sentence fragments.

The "call to action" tells the listener what she should be
doing about all this information you've been giving her. It's almost always phrased as a direct command: "Shop at Sears."
"Pick some up on your way home tonight." "Don't miss it!"
Since it's a direct command, it has to sound like one. You can't
afford to sound timid or hesitant. That would be like a door-to-
door salesman saying, "You don't want to buy any encyclopedias
today, do you? No, never mind. I'm sure you don't. I shouldn't
have bothered you." Be decisive and authoritative.

"The Super Bowl! Tomorrow!" "Bloomingdale's—
terrific." You can encounter such sentence fragments anywhere
in a piece of copy, but you'll find them most frequently in the final sentence or two—either alone or combined with a call-to-
action. The best way to approach sentence fragments, wherever
they occur, is to pretend you are answering an unspoken question. Imagine someone saying to you, "I forgot, so tell me again.
What's the name of this wonderful program you want me to
watch?" You answer this imagined question aloud, "Family
Feud." Again, the imagined voice: "And when can I see it?"

Again you say aloud, "Weeknights." Imagined: "What station?"
You: "Right here on Channel Four."

V – Technical Copy Problems

Piggyback Spots

Sometimes a sponsor will buy a block of time—say, sixty
seconds—and split it in half, running a spot for one of their products in the first thirty seconds and a spot for another product in
the second. For example, Lipton might run two spots back-to-
back; one for their instant iced tea mix and the other for Cup-a-
Soup. Or Kraft Foods might run a commercial for mayonnaise
followed immediately by one for Philadelphia Brand cream
cheese. In the advertising industry, these are referred to as *piggyback* spots. The only difference between piggybacks and any
other spot is how they are scheduled when they are put on the air.
They are designed to stand alone, and it really doesn't make
much difference what spots, if any, precede or follow them. Since
each spot is produced independently, the people producing
them, including the voice-over performer, have no idea how they
will be aired and proceed as they would for any other spot.

There is another type of piggyback spot you should be
aware of. This kind of piggyback is invariably for a sponsor who
sells two kinds of products; shoes and hats, for example. He wants
to get the most out of his advertising dollar, so he decides to talk
about both products in a single commercial. The wisdom of such
a decision, in terms of advertising effectiveness, is questionable.
But it does happen, and you should know how to handle such
spots when you encounter them.

If the spot talks about both hats and shoes throughout the spot, go ahead and treat it as you would any other spot. If, however, the spot deals with hats in the first part and, midway, switches the subject to shoes, look at it as though it were two distinct spots. Analyze each one. Decide what approach is appropriate to each and don't be surprised if your approach to the hat part of the script is different from the way you treat the shoe part.

The Copy Layout Trap

Copywriters sometimes lay out their copy as though it were a poem with specific lines and stanzas. Look at the Koni Shock Absorber spot in the sample copy section for an example of this kind of copy layout. When you see copy laid out this way, it should be an immediate warning to you to avoid getting locked into the interpretation that is suggested by the layout. The copywriter is trying to indicate how he heard it in his head as he wrote it. But you, as the professional performer, might be able to find an even more effective way of delivering the spot by deliberately ignoring the layout. In the Koni spot, for instance, you may decide that the three lines, "Less body lean . . . More stability, Crisper handling," should be treated as one line without any pauses between them. However, unless you are alert to the danger of the poetic layout, it might never occur to you to try such an interpretation.

The Koni spot also illustrates another common problem of copy layout: the three little dots called an *ellipsis*. Strictly speaking, an ellipsis should only be used when one or more words have been omitted from a quotation (as in the quote from *Alice in Wonderland* at the beginning of this chapter). In common practice, though, those three little dots crop up everywhere. Mostly, you'll find them wherever the copywriter thought would be a good place to pause; an example is after the phrase "Less body lean . . ."

Remember, although the copywriter is the expert on what words to choose and how to put them together, you are the expert on how to *say* those words. You can be sure if the copywriter were as skilled as you in *reading* copy, he would be reading the spot himself instead of hiring you to do it. So don't feel compelled to pause every time you see an ellipsis. You'll often find that the most effective reading is to ignore those three little dots.

In his highly acclaimed book *The Responsive Chord,* commercial creator and media expert Tony Schwartz gives an excellent example of how the way a piece of written copy is laid out on the page can influence the way we perceive the meaning of the copy and how, all too frequently, we can be seduced into reading it that specific way.

Two years ago I left the Superior Court to run for governor. At that time, I said I would be careful with the taxpayer's pocketbook, and I kept my word. I said I would improve the quality of government, and I kept my word. I said I would work in the best interests of both industry and labor, and I kept my word. I said I would deal with drug abuse, and I kept my word. I said I would do more to control crime, and I kept my word. In all of these things, what I've said, I've done, and I kept my word. This, to me, is what being governor is all about.

Two years ago I left the Superior Court to run for governor. At that time,

I said I would be careful with
the taxpayer's pocketbook, and
I kept my word.

I said I would improve the quality
of government, and I kept my word.

I said I would work in the best
interests of both industry and labor,
and I kept my word.

I said I would deal with drug abuse,
and I kept my word.

I said I would do more to control
crime, and I kept my word.

In all of these things, what I've said, I've done, and I kept my
word. This, to me, is what being governor is all about.

Two years ago I left the
Superior Court to run for
governor.

At that time, I said
I would be careful with
the taxpayer's pocketbook, and...........................I kept my word.

I said I would improve
the quality of government, and ....I kept my word.

I said I would work
in the best interests of
both industry and labor, and ....I kept my word.

I said I would deal
with drug abuse, and ....I kept my word.

I said I would do
more to control crime, and.....................,.............I kept my word.

In all of these things,
what I've said, I've done, and...........................I kept my word.

This, to me, is what being
governor is all about.

—— LISTEN TO CUT 4 ON THE INSTRUCTIONAL TAPE which will illustrate one way these three layouts might result in different readings.

What to Emphasize and What Not

I–Importance of Emphasis in Conveying Meaning

In normal face-to-face speech, we rely on a number of things other than the voice to carry meaning: facial expressions, gestures and other body language. But with voice-overs, we are robbed of these valuable tools and are forced to convey all of the meaning with only the voice. So we are limited, in the way we convey our meaning, to two things: the words we use and the way we say them. Unfortunately for us, we have no discretion in the choice of words. They are handed to us and we are stuck with them. The only option we have is to decide *which* words we emphasize and *how* we choose to emphasize them. These choices are the essence of the voice-over art.

To illustrate the importance of proper emphasis, take the sentence "I wasn't sure she broiled the lamb chop." Think for a moment about which words you would emphasize in this sentence. Now LISTEN TO CUT **5** ON THE INSTRUCTIONAL TAPE to see how many different meanings can be wrung out of the same sentence simply by emphasizing different words.

Tony Schwartz, in *The Responsive Chord,* provides us with another example of the importance of proper emphasis when he points out that " '*big* house' does not indicate the same thing as 'big *house*' or '*big-house.*' The first indicates a house that is big; the second, a big *house* as opposed to a big *bridge* or a big *tree;* the third, a prison."

We can see, therefore, how important it is, in conveying the intended meaning, to stress the proper words. But the questions still remain: "How does one decide which words to emphasize and which ones not to emphasize? And, when faced with the problem of choosing between more than one possible reading, each with stress on different words, how can one be sure of making the best decision?" Fortunately, there are some techniques which, when carefully learned and properly applied, can help us to make these decisions.

II – Content Words

Linguists frequently divide words into two categories: *content words* and *function words.* Content words carry meaning about the subject under discussion while function words tell us about the relationship between the content words. For example, take the familiar phrase "Now is the time for all good men to come to the aid of their party." The content words in this sentence are: now, time, all, good, men, aid, and party. All the other words are function words in that they tell us what the connection is between the content words. Take "now" and "time." What is the relationship between these two words? It's not that now *might be* or *could be* the time. Rather, we know conclusively that it *is* the time. Moreover, we know that it isn't just any old time or even one of several possible times. A function word distinctly tells us that it is *the* time.

As a general rule, content words are stressed or emphasized while function words are not. In the phrase "Now is the time" it would sound quite all right to stress only the words "now" and "time." But if you were to stress "is" the implication would be that there had been some question as to whether now really is the time or not. By emphasizing "is" you would imply, not only that such a question exists, but also that those who believe that now is not the time are in error and you forcefully expound your belief that now indeed *is* the time.

By incorrectly stressing the function word "is" you also create another problem. The stress placed on "is" robs strength from the content words "now" and "time." That would be perfectly acceptable if we already had been talking about whether now was or wasn't the time. But these are brand new ideas that nobody has heard in our discussion before. They have to be stressed in order to be established in the listener's mind. This necessity—of making sure the listener catches on to each new idea that's introduced into the discussion—each new content word—is the reason for using the next technique for determining which words need to be stressed and which do not.

III — Establishing the Subject

In the previous section we said that, in general, content words are stressed and function words are not. There are, however, many exceptions to that rule. The most valuable technique in determining which content words to stress is referred to as *establishing the subject*. The name derives from the fact that whenever a new subject or content word is introduced, it must be stressed in order to firmly establish it in the listener's mind. However, once a subject has been established, it is no longer necessary to keep on emphasizing it. A content word which appears in the first sentence should be stressed. Should the same word appear in any subsequent sentence, it is *not* stressed because it has already been established. Each time a content word appears for the first time, stress it; then forget it. If it's been established once, it doesn't need to be stressed again. As was pointed out about function words, incorrectly stressing a content word that has already been established robs strength from surrounding words that need to be emphasized, and it can cause the listener to infer a meaning that you did not intend.

To see more clearly how one establishes the subject, let's look at a piece of typical commercial copy. Read the Savarin Decaffeinated spot on the next page.

In preparing such a piece of copy, we need to go through it thought by thought, see what needs to be emphasized, what shouldn't be emphasized and, most important of all, *why.*

As we learned last chapter, the first thing to do with a piece of copy is analyze it by asking the four basic questions. Since a previous assignment included analyzing the Savarin spot, we will assume that you already know who your listener is, what she looks like (if you decided to speak to a woman), her age, marital status, family situation, education, and income level. We can't stop there, though; we have to understand how she is thinking while we are talking to her. We have to remember that she does not hear our spot as an isolated message. Rather, she perceives a commercial as merely a single link in a continuous chain of audio events. Before our spot started she may have heard a commercial for automobile tires and a weather forecast. Her mind is occupied, now, by deciding if she should wear a sweater and whether she should replace the rear tires on her car since the treads are almost worn away. She's also wondering if she should take an umbrella with her.

With your very first words, you must, metaphorically,

<table>
<tr><td rowspan="2">"EQUAL RIGHTS"</td><td>CLIENT ___Savarin Decaffeinated_____</td></tr>
</table>

"EQUAL RIGHTS"	CLIENT Savarin Decaffeinated
	MEDIA :50 Radio
	DATE 1/21/82
	JOB NO SCS-257 Rev. 1

CODE #SCS-126-50R

Savarin believes that all coffee drinkers should have equal rights. Even if you prefer decaffeinated coffee, you have a right to a delicious cup of coffee. And the right to pay a reasonable price for it.

With Savarin Decaffeinated you get everything you want from good coffee without the caffeine. Or the high price. Savarin Decaffeinated, vacuum can or instant, is less expensive than most other decaffeinated coffees. And that's good grounds for anyone to switch to Savarin.

Flavor is the other reason. Savarin makes their decaffeinated just as satisfying as their regular coffee. It has a taste that's so delicious and rich it would please the palate of the most discriminating coffee drinker. That's because Savarin uses only the finest coffee beans. After all, Savarin Decaffeinated is the coffee of El Exigente. And El Exigente, the Demanding One, would have it no other way.

So when it comes to decaffeinated coffee, why not be like El Exigente. Always demand the best—Savarin Decaffeinated.

take your listener by the lapels, stand nose-to-nose with her, stare firmly into her eyes and forcefully say: "Savarin! That's what we're talking about now! Forget sweaters and tires and umbrellas! It's Savarin, now! OK? You with me? Savarin! Right?"

With that in mind, it should be obvious that the first word in the Savarin spot should be stressed. Emphasizing the word "Savarin" establishes the subject for the entire spot. Incidentally, it's the name of the sponsor's product, and since in any spot the name of the product is certainly something we want to establish in the listener's mind, the product name is *always* stressed the first time it appears in a spot.

The next words to be established in this first thought (which, in this case, happens to also be the first sentence) are "all" and "coffee"; the final important words are "equal" and "rights."

Now, few people would argue that "Savarin," "all," "coffee" and "equal rights" are important ideas to get across to our listener. But what about all those other words? Somebody might feel that some other word or words should also be emphasized. So let's look at each of the other words and see why it should be left as an unstressed word.

If we emphasize "believes" we would imply that although *we* believe it, there may be some argument against our position and we might actually be wrong (a possibility we don't want to have cross the listener's mind for even the slightest fraction of a second). "That" is unquestionably a function word. We don't want to stress "drinkers" because it would rob strength from the stress we've just put on "coffee," and besides, it would imply that only coffee *drinkers* have equal rights but that coffee *roasters,* say, or coffee *grinders* don't. If you stressed the word "should" you would be implying that just prior to your speaking, someone else had declared that all coffee drinkers should *not* be entitled to equal rights. In righteous indignation, you rise up to declare that, indeed, they most certainly *should*! Similarly, if you were to stress the word "have" you would imply that someone else had asserted that some other verb might be more appropriate—perhaps just "know about" or, maybe, "be allowed to read about" equal rights instead of "having" them, and you're setting them straight.

So much for the first sentence. Now, let's move on to the second. Decaffeinated coffee is an important idea to get across, but the word coffee has already been established so the only word needing emphasis here is "decaffeinated." The only other word we need to stress in the second sentence is "delicious." One might be able to make a case for stressing "even" but it would be a weak case at best because the sentence reads smoothly and easily, and it actually sounds more conversational without stressing this word and we don't really lose any meaning. The general rule regarding content words is that you should stress only those words that absolutely need it. Put another way: emphasize as few words as possible. Putting emphasis on more words than necessary leads to an unnatural, sing-songy sound. "You" should not be stressed because to do so would imply that the listener had this right, but others didn't. That would be contradicting ourselves since we've already stated our firm conviction that all coffee drinkers should have equal rights. "Right" has already been established as has "coffee" and all the others are unquestionably pure function words.

If this copy had been written by a strict grammarian, he would not have put a period after the phrase "delicious cup of coffee." Instead, he would have used a comma and used a lowercase letter "a" to begin the word "and" making it one very long compound sentence. But this copywriter has, fortunately for us, set up each new thought as though it were a separate sentence. Remember, though, that not all copywriters are so obliging; we may have to redo the punctuation in order to properly convey the correct meaning.

In the third sentence, the only words which should be stressed are "reasonable price." Just as with the word "even" above, one might be able to make a case for stressing "and" but, as with "even" in the second sentence, it reads well without the stress; in fact, it sounds more conversational without it. Since there is no loss of meaning, we apply the principle that less is more and opt for not stressing it. "Pay" isn't stressed because, as with "should" in the first sentence, emphasis on "pay" would imply that there was a right to pay, but not to do something else— perhaps barter or steal a cup of coffee.

The two cases above—"Should" and "pay"—illustrate a general rule: Never stress verbs. That's it: verbs should *never* be stressed. Never? Ever? Well...there *is* one exception.

IV – Comparisons and Contrasts

There is a single rule, overriding all others, which requires us to stress a word that otherwise would never be stressed: *Words in comparison or contrast to each other are always stressed.* Even if it is an already established subject, even if it is a verb, even if it is a personal pronoun (we'll get into that shortly), if it is a case of comparison or contrast, you *have to* stress the words.

The dictionary defines "comparison" as "the juxtaposing of items to establish similarities and dissimilarities." "Contrast" is defined as "to compare in order to show unlikenesses or differences; note the opposite natures, purposes, etc., of." They mean almost the same thing except for the fact that contrasts always show differences and comparisons can also show similarities. We include both terms only because we want to be comprehensive.

Suppose we had been talking about pain relievers. We have already mentioned both aspirin and Anacin, so those subjects have been established and, following the rule, when they appear again in the copy, they should not be emphasized. Then we encounter the sentence, "Anacin has been proven to work twice as fast as aspirin." Now we have to stress both words—Anacin and aspirin—even though they have already been established.

Of course, the names of the products are not the only things that will be compared and contrasted. Almost any pair of words that point out the difference between one thing and another can qualify for the category of comparison and contrast and, thus, for stress. "Anacin is fast acting and gentle to your stomach." We are no longer comparing Anacin with another product. Instead, we are comparing two different attributes of Anacin: the facts that it acts quickly and that doesn't irritate your stomach.

When you spot a comparison, immediately look for another. More often than not, comparisons and contrasts occur, not as one word compared with another single word, but as comparisons of pairs of words. "Ordinary aspirin contains only 250 milligrams of pain relief. But Anacin gives you 500 milligrams." Here, aspirin is still compared to Anacin, but 250 is also compared with 500 so all four words must be stressed in order to emphasize both comparisons. Comparisons don't only come in pairs; they can also come in triplets. "Pleasant tasting, fast acting and longer lasting." We have a comparison between pleasant, fast and longer, and a comparison between tasting, acting and lasting. All six words should be stressed. Of course, they won't all be stressed the same way.

Now, reread the spot for Savarin Decaffeinated. See how many comparisons and contrasts you can find. Remember, you are looking for *explicit* contrasts. Don't get so engrossed in looking for subtle, hidden, implied contrasts that you overlook the obvious ones.

You probably noticed quite quickly that in the eleventh line of the copy a comparison is made between Savarin's decaffeinated coffee and their regular coffee. The word "regular" has not been used yet so it would have been stressed in any event. But the word "decaffeinated" has been abundantly established by this point in the copy. Under other circumstances, we wouldn't dream of stressing it. But because there is a comparison between decaffeinated and regular, both words need to be emphasized.

There are a number of other comparisons and contrasts you should have found in the Savarin spot.

First paragraph: decaffeinated—delicious
Second paragraph: caffeine—high price
               vacuum can—instant
               Savarin—other
Third paragraph: decaffeinated—regular

If you missed any of these, don't be disappointed; most people will miss one or more of them on the first reading. This piece of copy illustrates how common comparisons and contrasts are in advertising copy, and also how important it is for you to identify them. It takes time and effort, it takes several readings, it takes serious thinking about the meaning of the spot before you can find all the comparisons and contrasts. But it is important that you do a careful study of every piece of copy you encounter to locate them. Unless you know where the comparisons and contrasts are, you won't be able to properly emphasize them and unless you do that, you will not convey to your listener all the meaning intended by the copywriter.

V – Closings

In the final few sentences of a commercial, we have to change our rules about establishing new subjects because the last sentences sum up all we've been talking about. They are our last chance to make our point and to burn into the listener's memory the salient points of our argument. So we want to reestablish the points we have already made by emphasizing them again. Most important of all, it is our last chance to impress the product's name on the listener. So, no matter how many times we've mentioned the name before, the last time you say it, you should stress it. Hard! As an example of how already established words should be treated in a closing, look at the last paragraph in the Savarin spot.

We have been talking for almost an entire minute about decaffeinated coffee, so both words should certainly be established by now. But, since this is the last time we get to say the words, "decaffeinated" and "coffee" are both stressed. "El Exigente" was just mentioned a couple of lines earlier—not just once, but twice. Still, this is the ending and the last chance to get it across, so we stress "El Exigente." (Incidentally, the name is pronounced: El Ex-ee-*hen*-tay.) The word "best" is, at this late point in the copy, a brand new idea. All through the spot we have been saying that Savarin Decaffeinated is good coffee, but nowhere have we claimed that it is the very best. Since it is a new subject we have to establish it by stressing it. Of course, even if we had mentioned it previously, we'd still want to emphasize "best" because this is our summary. The final two words, "Savarin Decaffeinated," summarize the entire spot and are our last chance to impress the product name on the listener's mind. We deliberately and with great pride rest our case with the name of our glorious product, *Savarin Decaffeinated.*

VI–Multi-Word Names

The last two words of the Savarin spot illustrate a common occurrence: a product name that consists of more than one word. It's important to remember in such cases that each word must be given equal stress. If we were to only stress the first word— *Savarin* Decaffeinated—it would imply a comparison with some other brand of decaffeinated coffee and, quite frankly, we'd just as soon the listener not even be aware there *are* any other decaffeinated brands. On the other hand, if we were to only stress the second word—Savarin *Decaffeinated*—we would imply a comparison with Savarin's regular coffee. And since we just said our product is the best, we would be implying the regular coffee our sponsor makes is, somehow, inferior to the decaffeinated version—certainly not at all what our sponsor would want to hear. So, when faced with a product name containing two or more words, give equal stress to each of the words. One more example will make the point even clearer. Suppose the product in question is Lysol Laundry Sanitizer, a relatively new addition to the Lysol line of products and a new kind of laundry powder that is used along with regular detergent to kill germs. By stressing only the word "Lysol"—*Lysol* Laundry Sanitizer—you would imply a comparison with some other brand of laundry sanitizer. Yet, it's a brand-new product, and so far Lysol is the only brand on the market. To stress "Laundry"—Lysol *Laundry* Sanitizer—would imply a comparison with Lysol's other kinds of sanitizers. But although Lysol does make other products, such as disinfectants and disinfectant sprays, they do not make any other products called sanitizers. Finally, if we stress "Sanitizer"—Lysol Laundry *Sanitizer*—we imply a comparison with Lysol's other laundry products—their detergent, perhaps, or their spray starch.

VII – How to Emphasize

After all this talk about what words should be emphasized and what words shouldn't, an understandable question might be: "Just what is meant by 'emphasize'? How, exactly, do you go about stressing a word?" The dictionary defines emphasis as "a particular prominence given in reading or speaking to one or more words or syllables." In voice-overs, we always relate our work to our listener. So we might say, for our purposes, that emphasis consists of doing something in the way we read a piece of copy to make a particular word stand out with particular prominence in the listener's mind. Some of the most common things a speaker can do to put emphasis on a particular word are:

1. PUNCH—Simply say the word with more force or volume. In other words, say it louder. Punching a word is, by far, the most common way to convey emphasis.

2. SAY IT SOFTER—A few years ago, Catherine Deneuve was featured in a commercial in which she delivered the now famous line, "If you want someone to listen to what you have to say . . . *whisper!*" Deneuve was absolutely right. Just as saying a word louder can call attention to that word, so can saying it softer. In fact, anything about the way you say a word that makes it stand

out from the other words in a sentence will place emphasis on that word in your listener's mind. You don't have to actually whisper in order to stress a word, you can just say it more softly and you will achieve the desired emphasis.

In fact, in most cases, you don't want to really whisper at all. You actually want to use what is called a "stage whisper." With an actual whisper, all of the voice is lost and what remains is only the whooshing or hissing sound produced by air passing over the tongue and teeth. Without some vocalization, almost all the sound's personality is lost. Unless the vocal chords are vibrating, you can't tell one voice from another; all whispers sound the same. So when you want to achieve the effect of a whisper, don't go all the way. Keep some voice in it by half-whispering and half-talking. You want to continue to use your voice, but with a very soft, very breathy tone.

For an example of what a stage whisper sounds like, please LISTEN TO CUT 6 ON THE INSTRUCTIONAL TAPE.

3. PAUSE SLIGHTLY—Deneuve proved her point by almost whispering the word "whisper," but she also did something else to heighten the stress on the word. She put a very slight pause before the word. This is quite an effective technique if carefully and sparingly used. The pause should be just the slightest hesitation, not a full end-of-paragraph stop. The pause must always come *before* the word to be stressed. The reason this technique works is that it interrupts the even flow of words at a point where the listener is not expecting an interruption and, as such, calls his attention to what he is hearing. A pause after the word does no good since a pause or hesitation always calls attention to the next word spoken.

As with all techniques for emphasis, except punching a word, pauses should be used very sparingly. One pause in a spot can work well. In a sixty second spot you may be able to get away with it a second time, but more than that is really pushing your luck. The technique of pausing for emphasis can be easily overused, and by doing so you run a real risk of sounding affected rather than effective. All these techniques rely on their novelty to grab the listener's attention. Once she catches on to what's happening, much like a person who has figured out how the magician's trick works, your listener won't tumble for it any more.

4. VARY SPEED—Saying a word or phrase faster or slower can add stress to that word. Words like "quick" and phrases like "in an instant" are made more effective if they are said quickly. Words like "slowly" and phrases like "longer lasting" can convey a stronger meaning if actually said more slowly.

5. WORD COLORING—Varying the speed at which you say a word according to the word's meaning is just one example of word coloring. This is related to, but not the same as onomatopoeia, which refers to words that in and of themselves sound like their referent, such as "cuckoo" or "buzz" or "boom." Word coloring consists of *saying* the word in a way that corresponds to the word's meaning. A word like "power" should be said powerfully. "Rough" can be said roughly and "smoother" can be said smoothly. Say "hearty" in a hearty tone of voice and "soothing" in a soothing tone. "Happy" should sound happy, "sad" should sound sad and when you say "proud" stick out your chest and sound full of pride.

—— LISTEN TO CUT **7** ON THE INSTRUCTIONAL TAPE.

6. NON-VERBAL SOUNDS—If you see "Mmmmmmmm" on a script, they don't want you to hum. They want you to make the same kind of sound you would naturally make if you took a bite of something that tasted incredibly good. You might even add a little bit of lip-smacking.

A slight chuckle at just the right time can be quite effective but, like the use of pauses for emphasis, it can be easily overdone. A few years ago, Victor Kiam, the owner of Remington Razor Co., decided to do his own television commercials. In an attempt to sound friendly and sociable, Kiam peppered his delivery with little chuckles. Instead of portraying affability, though, he came across as phony and insincere. Fortunately, Kiam has stopped overusing the chuckle and the change has been to his advantage.

No matter how good a voice-over person is, campaigns change, styles change, and a perfectly good performer may be replaced for no better reason than somebody felt it was time for a change. As of the writing of this book, television commercials for Taster's Choice Coffee are being voiced by Hugh Morgan, one of the hottest and most talented voice-over performers in New York. For years, though, all Taster's Choice spots were voiced by veteran Chicago announcer, Ken Nordine. Nordine made his reputation largely on the way he said one word: "Ahhh!" Technically, "ahhh!" isn't a word at all, but a nonverbal sound. No matter what it is, when Nordine said it, you just knew the man was a confirmed coffeeholic. The satisfaction he was able to get into that one sound was infectious, and was responsible, as much as any other factor, for selling literally tons of instant coffee.

Another nonverbal sound that can be quite effective is a sigh. In her song, "In My Tennessee Mountain Home," Dolly Parton hit upon a very evocative phrase: "life's as peaceful as a baby's sigh." Granted, a baby's sigh can evoke strong feelings. But a sigh from just about anyone can be effective in conveying to the listener feelings of peace and contentment. Depending on how it is used, it could also convey sadness or resignation.

7. USE BODY LANGUAGE—The introduction to this book pointed out how voice-over performers can't rely on facial expressions, gestures or other body language to convey meaning; the listener has only your voice from which to extract the meaning of the copy. But that doesn't mean you should avoid using body language while you are reading copy aloud. On the contrary, body language can play an important role in helping you put more meaning into what you do with your voice. Throughout our lives we have been accustomed to using certain facial expressions, certain postures, certain gestures when we feel a specific emotion

and express corresponding feelings. So it's not too surprising that when we use those gestures and expressions and when we adopt those postures, it's easier for us to express the emotions with which they are associated. While you are reading copy, don't hesitate to use body language and hand gestures. When you punch a word, punch the air with your fist. When you're trying to sound proud, stand tall and grasp your lapels. When you're trying to sound soothing, make soothing gestures with your hands. If you stand rigid and straight with your hands at your sides, unmoving, your voice will sound equally rigid and stilted. So let yourself go. Point your finger. Wave your arms. Get carried away. So long as you don't make any extraneous noise doing it, it can only help you in your delivery.

Common Problems

Many years ago when you were in the first grade, your teacher said something like, "All right, class. Today we are going to read. Mary, stand up please and read the first page." Little Mary stood up and read, word by word: "Look! Look and see! See Dick? See Jane? See Dick and Jane run! Run, Dick. Run, Jane. See Puff and Spot? See Puff and Spot run after Dick and Jane. Funny, funny Puff. Funny, funny Spot." As she read aloud, Mary carefully pronounced each word separately. She didn't even think about conveying what little meaning there was in the material she had to read. She was totally concerned with getting the words right—never mind what the words meant. And that's a pity because to this day, whenever she has to read aloud, grown woman Mary becomes much more concerned with saying each word than she is with conveying meaning.

Countless scholars have written about how language started out as a verbal medium. Only after millions of years was writing devised as a way to represent and preserve verbal speech. At first, writing was a pretty loose business. People spelled things the way they sounded to them, and punctuation was sketchy, when it existed at all. Gradually, as society became more organized, writing became more standardized. Rules were laid down for grammar and spelling. Writing, which had first been descriptive, in that it described the way people actually spoke, slowly became prescriptive in that it prescribed the "proper" way language *should* be used. Spoken language, of course, kept evolving, but written language and its rules calcified and a gap appeared between the written and spoken forms. Today, many of the rules of written grammar, if they ever did apply to spoken language, no longer do. In some parts of the world, and in some social classes, this gap is wider than in others. The considerable divergence between the way words are written and how they are pronounced in the French language is an excellent example of how spoken and written language can become disconnected.

Sometimes the rules are so intimidating that, instead of causing a split between written and spoken language, the rules for writing limit the way the language is spoken. As Marshall McLuhan has pointed out, British upper-class speech does quite a good job of imitating printed language. It is monotonous in its almost total lack of variation in rhythm and inflection—especially when compared with largely nonwritten brogues like Scottish and Irish and, in America, rural southern and black dialects. McLuhan sees the musical quality of these dialects as accounting for the extraordinary musical talent of the peoples who speak them. Moreover, he points out that by mimicking printed language in their speech patterns, the British upper class maintains its position in the class structure. In the opening song of Lerner and Loewe's *My Fair Lady*, Professor Henry Higgins complains, "An Englishman's way of speaking absolutely classifies him. The moment he talks he makes some other Englishman despise him."

In addition to the problem of the difference between spoken and written language, there is another, probably even more fundamental, problem with trying to read written words aloud. When you speak extemporaneously, your mind is solely concerned with the ideas you are trying to convey. You may hesitate momentarily to search your vocabulary for precisely the right word. But, other than that, the speech process is completely automatic. Not for the slightest instant do you think about the mechanics of what you are saying. It never crosses your mind that you have just completed a grammatical sentence and should pause before starting another. No, you keep plowing along until you have finished the thought you wanted to convey. You don't impose upon yourself arbitrary requirements to end all questions with a rising inflection and all declarative sentences with a falling one. Of course not! You instinctively use whatever inflection is appropriate to the content of what you are saying.

When the thoughts aren't your own, though—when you have to use words chosen by someone else—the automatic processes break down. That's why we have put so much emphasis on analyzing the copy to determine the copywriter's original intent. Unless you understand the idea behind the copy and make an active effort to communicate that idea, you revert to a polished and sophisticated version of what you did in grade school: just reading words.

Experience has shown that there are a number of things people tend to do when reading someone else's words that they would never do when speaking extemporaneously. All these things convey a subliminal impression to the listener that you aren't really speaking *to* him, but are reading *at* him. Since our goal is to achieve a pseudo-conversational style, we should know about these things and train ourselves to avoid them.

1—Down Endings and Patterning

You might recall your first grade teacher putting a dot on the blackboard and telling the class, "This is a period. It comes at the end of a sentence and when you see a period, your voice should go down." Well, sometimes yes. But many times, it's better, more natural sounding to use an up inflection. Look at the first sentences of the Koni and Home Pride spots. Try reading them aloud; first with a downward inflection on the last word and then with a rising inflection.

WHEN TENDER YOUNG TURKEY IS BASTED WITH BUTTER, YOU CAN PRACTICALLY TASTE IT WITH YOUR EYES.

ONE SHOCK ABSORBER IS SO SUPERIOR IT HAS BEEN USED BY EVERY WORLD CHAMPION FOR THE PAST 13 YEARS.

—— LISTEN TO CUT **8** ON THE INSTRUCTIONAL TAPE.

As you can see, a period doesn't always mean a downward inflection. Still, many—probably most—declarative and imperative sentences sound best with a downward inflection on the final syllable of the last word, because that's the way we actually do it in normal extemporaneous conversation.

There is, however, another problem associated with downward inflections. It's a persistent pattern of inflection that starts the phrase on a relatively high inflection and with each few words drops the inflection lower. Graphically, it would be represented most nearly as resembling a descending staircase.

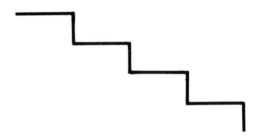

Perhaps this kind of down ending is caused by the fact that the eye has already perceived the end coming up and the mind has started too soon to prepare for it. Whatever the reason, the down ending syndrome never occurs as an isolated instance; it is always a *repeating* pattern that is boring, monotonous and gives the listener the inescapable impression that you are reading at him.

Like the small-station lilt, discussed in Chapter 2, the down ending does not correspond to any speech pattern in normal conversation. The hard part, in both the case of down endings and small-station lilt, is realizing that you are doing it and being able to hear it when listening to your own playback.

─── LISTEN TO CUT **9** ON THE INSTRUCTIONAL TAPE.

I I – Q u e s t i o n s

After the first grade teacher told you every period requires a down ending, he put something on the blackboard that looked like this: ? "That," he told the class, "is a question mark. Every time you see a question mark, you should make your voice go up." Well, sometimes that's true. But not all the time. In fact, not even most of the time.

After all these years, somebody is finally going to tell you the correct rule—a rule corresponding to what we actually do in extemporaneous speech. Here it is: *with short questions that can be answered by either "yes" or "no," use an up inflection.* "Want high interest for your money?" "Want absolute safety for your savings?" Up inflections.

But that's only half the rule. Here's the rest of it: *with all other questions, use a down inflection on the final syllable.* A question you can't answer with a simple "yes" or "no" is usually a rhetorical question, since the speaker doesn't actually expect an answer from the listener. Rhetorical questions are really declarative sentences in disguise, and almost all declarative sentences are best read with a down ending on the final syllable. "What would you say if I told you it's possible to get high interest rates for your savings along with absolute safety for your money?" The speaker doesn't care one whit what you would say if he told you what he's already told you. He's simply telling you what he's telling you and the question form—"what would you say if I told you . . ."—is simply a rhetorical device to introduce the actual sentence. You could cut it off and the sentence wouldn't loose a bit of its meaning. It's really a declarative sentence. Down inflection!

Even if you *can* answer "yes" or "no," a sentence that runs on for any length should not end with an up inflection because, invariably, it will prove to also be a rhetorical question. "Have you ever wondered if your savings account is giving you the highest interest rate allowed by law along with the safety of a federally insured account?" Down ending! "But," you say, "it ends with a question mark and it can be answered 'yes' or 'no.'" Doesn't matter! It's too long, so end it with a down inflection on the final syllable.

—— LISTEN TO CUT **10** ON THE INSTRUCTIONAL TAPE.

III—Listings

When more than two items appear in sequence, you have a list. It can be three or more words or three or more phrases. "Quick, delicious, and economical." "Fast acting, medically effective, pleasant tasting." The key to handling listings is to avoid the monotony of saying each item in the list the same way. Instead, try to give a different reading to each item. Read one with an up inflection, another with an even inflection, and the third with a medium inflection. If the context of the words allows it, try word coloring. Especially with more than three items, a technique that might work well is the *build*. A build, as the name implies, is accomplished by starting at a relatively mild energy level and, with each subsequent item in the listing, increasing the energy. The danger with a build is that you might run out of energy before you run out of items in the list. So be sure you start with a low enough energy level to allow you to expand throughout the entire list. If the list is so long that you still can't read it believably, you might want to find a point in the build where you can logically change to some other technique. Or, you might want to use some other technique at first and switch to a build in the middle of the list. The important thing is to keep the elements in listings from all sounding the same.

Remember that listings frequently occur in pairs. When they do, you are almost always going to encounter a comparison or contrast. Even a single listing can contain comparisons and contrasts. When you encounter them, rely on the techniques we have already discussed for reading them.

—— LISTEN TO CUT II ON THE INSTRUCTIONAL TAPE.

IV – New Thoughts Need New Readings

Sometimes, a piece of copy is written as a homogeneous whole. The Home Pride spot is a good example. But other spots have sections that talk about different things—what acting instructors call "beats." Look at the Savarin spot again. The first paragraph talks about equal rights for people who like decaffeinated coffee. The second paragraph talks about low price. The third paragraph talks about flavor and the last paragraph, as we've already discussed, is the closing summary. When you make the transition from one thought to another, you must change the way you read the copy to signal to your listener that you are shifting ideas. You can change your inflection—if you ended high, start low; if you ended low, start high. You can vary the speed at which you read each section. You can also vary your energy level from section to section. If you recall our previous discussion of the introduction-elaboration-summary copy style, you'll recall that what we were really doing was varying the energy level as the copy changed from section to section. Whenever you introduce a whole new concept, do it with a new reading. After all, that's exactly what we do in normal conversation!

V – Unfriendly Tones

Back in Chapter 2 we talked about the qualities to strive for in doing voice-overs: pseudo-conversational, believable and non-intrusive. All of these qualities are impossible if you don't sound reasonably friendly. Yet some people, when reading copy, tend to sound hostile. Like other problems that crop up when you are working with someone else's words, unfriendly tones are something the speaker is unaware of until he hears himself on tape. Even then, he may not recognize what he's doing until it is pointed out to him. Be on the lookout for these common problems.

Patronizing

Think about how some adults talk to very small children. "Oh, *my!* Aren't you a *pretty* little girl! And *isn't* that a *pretty dress* you're wearing! Did your *mommy* make that dress?" They speak slower and louder than normal as though the child might be retarded or hard of hearing, and they overemphasize random words. This sort of speech pattern occasionally turns up when people try to read commercial copy. Perhaps it has something to do with their image of how they think an "announcer" should sound. The result is to sound as though they are patronizing the listener.

Antagonistic

Others, when reading copy, develop an antagonistic tone. It's as though they expect the listener to resist them and they have determined to ram their message down the listener's throat. It's quite amazing because the people who develop this problem, in normal conversation are frequently the nicest, least aggressive people you'd ever want to meet.

Lack of Warmth

When there's only a very slight tone of antagonism in a speaker's voice, it's sometimes referred to as a lack of *warmth*. In other words, it just doesn't sound friendly enough. Whether the problem is full-fledged antagonism or just a lack of warmth, there is a trick that can help solve the problem: smile! Purposely put a smile on your face and keep it there as you read the copy. It may sound dumb, but it really works. There are two reasons why; physically, smiling alters the structure of your mouth and, therefore, changes the way sound is formed as you speak. It may be a small change, but it's an important change. The second reason accounts for a much more profound effect on your delivery. In all your experience, whenever you have felt happy, gregarious, friendly, and outgoing you automatically smiled. At a very deep Pavlovian level you have come to associate these feelings with the position of your facial muscles while smiling. When you consciously put a smile on your face, you tend to feel more friendly and happy. According to the *New York Times*, research done at the University of California at San Francisco has shown the act of flexing facial muscles into characteristic expressions of various emotions, such as joy, can produce effects on the nervous system, including heartbeat, respiration, skin temperature and other vital involuntary functions, normally associated with those emotions.

You can prove to yourself how effective this trick can be. Put a smile on your face and hold it there. Then imagine you are cussing someone out. Say something like "You dirty, rotten, filthy S.O.B. I hate your lying guts!" So long as you keep the smile, there's simply no way you can sound as though you mean it.

Shakespeare, superb observer of human nature that he was, knew about this phenomenon. When preparing his men for battle, Shakespeare's King Henry V says:

> Stiffen the sinews, summon up the blood,
> Disguise fair nature with hard-favored rage;
> Then lend the eye a terrible aspect . . .
> Now set the teeth and stretch the nostril wide,
> Hold hard the breath and bend up every spirit
> To his full height.

Shakespeare knew that adopting the postures of particular emotions, whether they be courage, aggression or anger, would make it far easier to feel those emotions and would more easily lead one to acting them out.

—— LISTEN TO CUT **12** ON THE INSTRUCTIONAL TAPE.

VI–Personal Pronouns

Remember your basic English grammar? In case you've forgotten, the personal pronouns are, in the nominative case:

I, you, he, she, it, we, they and **one** (when used instead of **you**).

In the genitive case they are:

my, our, your, his, her, its, their and **one's**;

mine, ours, yours, hers, theirs.

In the accusative case they are:

me, you, him, her, it, us, them and **one.**

One of the most common mistakes people make when reading copy is to unnecessarily emphasize personal pronouns. By far the greatest offender, probably because it appears most often in commercials, is "you." Look at the Home Pride spot. In the first sentence, we see "When tender young turkey is basted with butter, you can practically taste it with your eyes." If you were to emphasize "you" you would be implying that someone else could not taste it—only "you," which bears no relationship to what you are really saying. Another objection to stressing "you" in this sentence is that by so doing you rob strength from the emphasis you need to put on the preceding word, "butter." And, as a clincher, "you" is not a content word, merely a function word and, you'll recall, we never put stress on a function word.

One reason people tend to stress the word "you" is that they are trying to say the word distinctly and don't realize that there are really two pronunciations for the word. What you normally think of when you see the word in print, and the only pronunciation listed in some smaller dictionaries is "yoo." But there is another, probably more frequently used pronunciation. The closest it can be approximated in print would be "yuh." But, the vowel sound is totally unstressed; practically absent. It's the same "you" that you hear when a valley girl says "you know"—it comes out more like "y'know." *Webster's New Collegiate* gives the pronunciation of the unstressed "you" as "yə." That upside down "e" is called a *schwa* and represents a reduced vowel, i.e., a vowel that receives the weakest level of stress (which can be thought of as no stress) within a word, as in the second syllable of the word telegraph.

In the Home Pride spot, the word "can" is also unstressed so the two words are combined into "y'cən." But be on guard for another common problem in regard to the word "can." The correct vowel sound for this word would rhyme with "pan" and "hand." It is perfectly acceptable and, in most cases preferable, when the word is unstressed to use a schwa for the vowel sound. Beware, however, of changing the "a" to an "i" sound so that it rhymes with "pin" or "tin" and comes out sounding like "kin" as in "kinfolk."

In like manner, many function words are not pronounced according to the dictionary. Since they are unstressed words, the vowel sounds become schwas. Don't feel compelled to give proper and complete vowel sounds for every word. The first thing you have to figure out is whether the word should be emphasized or not. Only then can you decide whether you need to give it the proper vowel sound or a schwa. Why? Because that's the way we do it in normal everyday conversation.

The ONLY Exception

We have said very dogmatically that you should never stress a personal pronoun. Like most immutable rules, this one has an exception. In Chapter 4 we said that there is one rule that overrides all others, in the sense that it requires us to stress a word that, otherwise, would never be stressed: words in comparison to or contrast with each other are always stressed. Look at the Koni spot. The next-to-last sentence contains a personal pronoun that must be stressed. "Put the world's finest performance shocks on *your* car." The first part of the spot tells us that Koni shocks are standard on Ferraris, Aston Martins, and Mustang SVOs. The implication is that since these shocks are good enough to be on these expensive cars, they should be used by you, too. The contrast is between these other cars and *your* car. In order to bring out that contrast you have to stress "you." Another obvious example: The Tri-State Chevy spot. "Let's talk about a couple of number ones. You and your Tri-State Chevrolet dealer." Without stress on "you" to bring out the comparison with the Chevy dealer, the spot wouldn't make too much sense. You have to stress both "you" and "Chevrolet dealer" to bring out the comparison. When you find yourself wanting to stress a personal pronoun, look to see if there is an explicit comparison or contrast. If there is, you're home free. If there isn't any way to justify the emphasis with a comparison or contrast, resist the urge.

The Other Personal Pronouns

So far, we've talked exclusively about the second person singular "you." But at the beginning of this section, we listed *all* the personal pronouns. The rule still holds: unless there is a case of comparison or contrast, *never* put stress on a personal pronoun.

As an example of the error of emphasizing personal pronouns even in other types of performance, in a recent Broadway production of *A Chorus Line*, an understudy was brought in to play the part of Cassie. It was obvious why she was only an understudy; she was terrible! Not that she wasn't beautiful and a terrific dancer and singer. But when she delivered her lines, she sounded stiff, wooden and unnatural. The major problem was that she kept stressing personal pronouns, particularly the first person singular. "When *I* came to New York, *I* decided that *I* wanted to be a star. So *I* went on auditions." Fortunately the word "I" rarely comes up in commercial copy. But you see that the rule is broader than just voice-over—an indication of its importance.

A personal pronoun that does frequently show up in commercial copy is "we" along with its variants, "our" and "us." It's not a very good writing style to have the announcer speaking as though he were a part of the sponsor's company, but you will encounter it and you should be warned: unless there is a comparison or contrast to justify the emphasis, never stress "we."

No matter what the personal pronoun, the rule still holds: except in the case of comparisons and contrasts, never stress a personal pronoun. On the other hand, if there *is* a comparison or contrast, you *must* stress the words compared or contrasted, even if they happen to be personal pronouns.

Common Objections

From time to time, people object to the rule on personal pronouns and, invariably, the objections they raise fall into one of
several common categories.

    1. "I want to personalize it for the listener." When you
think about this statement, you realize what it really means is you
want the listener to feel you are talking directly to him and to no
one else. But that is the goal of all voice-overs, and we accomplish
our goal by doing all the things we've talked about to make ourselves sound natural and conversational. Since we don't stress
personal pronouns in normal conversation, doing it while reading
copy won't make the listener feel we are talking directly to him;
on the contrary, it will subliminally give him the impression that
we are reading at him rather than talking to him.

    2. "I've heard people doing it on the air." Yes, you
have. And you've also heard people on the air doing a lot of other
terribly unprofessional things. People sometimes wind up doing
commercials for reasons other than the fact that they are good at
it. They may own the company. Their husband or their father
may own the company. They may be a good friend of the person
who owns the company. They may be a good friend of the person
who owns the advertising agency. They may be a good friend of
the producer. The producer may simply not know what he's doing. The list could go on for pages. Yes, you will hear people on
the air—people who, you think, must be good because they are
working—doing all sorts of things, including stressing personal
pronouns, that you have been taught are anathema to good voice-
overs. But the one thing you will never hear is one of the leaders
of the profession doing it. You may hear Frank Carvel or Berna-
dette Castro or the owner of the local auto dealership stressing
personal pronouns, but you'll never hear Mason Adams do it.
Nor will you hear Bob McFadden do it. Nor Peter Thomas, or
Dick Fonda, or Bob Landers, or Joyce Gordon, or Herb Hartig,
or Alan Blevis, or Cynthia Adler, or Fran Brill, or any of the top

professionals who have been working in the field for years and who will continue to work for years to come.

3. "It just doesn't sound right not to stress it" or "It sounds so much better when I stress it." If this is the way you feel, it should be a warning to you that one of two things has happened. It could very well be that there is a comparison or contrast you haven't noticed. Look for it. Carefully. If there definitely is no comparison that you've missed, it means that you are still carrying in your mind an idea of how you think "an announcer" should sound, and you are unconsciously using a patterned delivery that corresponds to that "announcerish" sound.

Implied Comparisons

On rare occasions, you'll encounter copy that is written to imply a comparison even though it doesn't state the comparison explicitly.

> TO EVERYBODY WHO PUTS IN A HARD DAYS WORK, THIS BUD'S FOR YOU. YEAH, JUST FOR YOU. THAT DISTINCTIVELY CLEAN CRISP TASTE THAT SAYS BUDWEISER. FOR ALL YOU DO, THIS BUD'S FOR YOU.

The implication is that all the other Buds are for other people, but this particular one is for you. There is simply no way to read this copy and make it make sense without stressing "you" because of the very strong implied comparison.

Note carefully the words "rare occasions" at the beginning of this section. The cases of true implied comparisons are so rare, this section was nearly left out of the book. Almost every time you think you can stress a pronoun because of an implied comparison, you will find, after thinking more about it, it's only an excuse to justify the "it sounds better this way" rationale. If the copy says something like "I want to talk for a minute to you, the guy who thinks his life isn't going anywhere," OK, you're obviously making a play for this one particular guy instead of all the others who may be listening. Go ahead and stress "you." But unless you can make such a clear distinction between the person you're talking to and all the other people who might be listening, it isn't an implied contrast. Leave it alone!

The Only OTHER Exception

There is one circumstance that will require you to ignore everything you have learned and stress a personal pronoun even though there is no comparison, no contrast and no legitimate justification for doing so anywhere in the copy—when the client insists on it. Rarely, if ever, will a good producer ask for such a reading, but not all producers are that good. Same goes for directors. So the day will come when you will be asked to do what you know is wrong. You have an obligation to give your clients the best, most professional, most natural, most conversational sounding reading you are capable of—on the first reading. If they insist on something else, give them what they want. After all, they're paying you to do what *they* want, not what you want.

VII—Articles

The Indefinite Articles

When reading aloud, some people tend to pronounce the article "a" as though it rhymed with "pay." But there is no such word. "A" pronounced that way is a letter of the alphabet, not a word. The word "a" is a schwa and is pronounced "uh." The other indefinite article, "an," likewise includes a schwa and is pronounced "uhn." It is always a mistake to be overprecise in pronunciation—more precise than we actually are in normal conversation.

The Definite Article

There are two pronunciations for the word "the." Before a word beginning with a vowel sound, it is pronounced "thee." Before a word beginning with a consonant sound, the proper pronunciation is "thuh." You would say "thee apple" and "thee oven" but would say "thuh book" or "thuh couch."

VIII—Numbers

Numbers keep cropping up in commercial copy. Mostly, it's prices. But they also appear as annual percentage rates, mileage figures, and various kinds of measurements. Look at the Gimbels spot. By now, it shouldn't surprise you that the key to handling numbers is to say them the way you would in normal conversation. You certainly wouldn't say "one-five percent" or "five-oh percent." What you'd say is "fifteen percent" or "fifty percent." When it comes to money, the water gets a little muddy because there's more than one way we normally talk about money. When you see a price written in digits instead of words, there's nothing to tell you how to say it. For example, "$59.99" could be said "fifty-nine, ninety-nine" or it could be said "Fifty-nine dollars and ninety-nine cents." Either is correct in the sense that we might naturally use either form in normal conversation. The choice has to be made by considering the type of product, the spirit of the copy, and the way the copy flows. In the Gimbels spot, the product is a common, everyday item, a vacuum cleaner. The copy is informally written with lots of exclamation points. So this copy would probably need "fifty-nine, ninety-nine." Another factor in favor of the shorter formulation is the fact that the copy is moderately dense; it's going to take a reasonably brisk pace to get everything said in less than thirty seconds. It takes longer to say "Fifty-nine dollars and ninety-nine cents" than it does to say "fifty-nine, ninety-nine." Since seconds literally count in commercials, save yourself some time by using the shorter version.

Another important thing to note about saying numbers is the use in the above example of the word "and." If you are using the longer formulation, the word "and" is the way you say the decimal point. This becomes important to remember when the numbers get above a hundred. Some people have a tendency to say "a hundred *and* sixty-four dollars," when it should be "a hundred, sixty-four dollars." It becomes even more of a problem with numbers above a hundred with cents added on. It would sound unwieldy to say the least, to say "a hundred *and* sixty-two dollars *and* ninety-eight cents." It is simpler and technically correct to always use "and" as the verbal equivalent of the decimal point and to never use it otherwise when dealing with numbers.

Still another problem with numbers: how do you say $150? Should you say "a hundred fifty dollars"? Or would it be correct, as some people do when reading copy, to say "one hundred fifty dollars"? To answer this, we, as usual, go back to what is done in informal conversation. If someone where to ask what you paid for your new watch, you might reply: "Oh, I got it for a hundred fifty dollars." You wouldn't normally go so far as to actually say "I got it for one hundred fifty dollars." To do so would imply a contrast with someone else who had to pay at least two hundred for their watch. And that leads to the one exception to this rule—as with all other rules about stress—when there is a comparison or contrast, use the "one hundred" form. If the copy tells how this watch normally sells for over two hundred dollars, but now it's available for only $189.99, you bring out that contrast by saying "*One* hundred eighty-nine dollars and ninety-nine cents" and even make it stronger by stressing "one." But that's the only situation where you would ever use the word "one" instead of "a" before "hundred." At all other times, the rule is to

convert the number "1" into the word "a" (pronounced "uh").
A hundred eighty-nine dollars and ninety-nine cents.

A similar rule holds for the verbalization of written fractions. If you tell your listener how all merchandise is four-fifths
off this weekend she might realize what a bargain is available and
rush right out to buy something. If, however, you tell her the merchandise is "one-fifth off," you are calling attention to the "one"
and the listener might wonder why the discount isn't two- or
three- or four-fifths. The rule on fractions is that wherever the numerator of the fraction (that's the number on top) is two or more,
you say the number. When the numerator is one, you say "a." A
fifth, a third, a half.* Again, the only exception is when there is a
comparison or contrast. The copy may talk about how everybody
else's costs have gone up by at least two-fifths while we have held
our increases to only one-fifth. Here we have an example of the
case where you would use "one" in the numerator of a fraction.

Remember, we are concerned here only with voice-
overs, and the goal of the voice-over person is to sound as natural
and believable as possible. Other people, like newscasters or
sportscasters, aren't interested in sounding conversational. They
want to sound like they know everything. Many of them are also
frightened someone might misunderstand something they say
and sue, so they go to great lengths to ensure what they say is
couched in the clearest, simplest terms possible. You will constantly hear newscasters use the "one hundred" formulation.
That's fine. When you get a job as a newscaster, you too can say
"one hundred" all you want. But while you're doing voice-overs,
restrain yourself. Just keep trying to sound conversational.

---

* Think of how unnecessary it is and how dumb it really sounds to say "one-
half." One is the only numerator you can have. You can't have two halves of something
because you'd then have a whole thing. You can't have three halves of something because you'd then have a whole and a half. Even the comparison exception can't apply
here because there isn't anything to compare it with. Since there can't possibly be any
comparison between one half and any other number of halves, there is never any reason to say "one"; it's *always* "a half."

IX – Choppiness

In the life of every good voice-over person comes the day when someone tells you "it sounds too choppy." What they're trying to tell you is that you have too many pauses in your delivery. It's another one of those things we tend to do when reading someone else's words and never do when extemporizing. In normal conversation, we begin with an idea. We take a big, healthy breath of air and start off. Usually we don't stop until we've finished the thought, or when we need to pause to search our memory for the right word to express the idea we have. With someone else's words on paper, however, too often we aren't concerned with the idea, just the words. Our eyes have a limited capacity to absorb print. So we stare at a group of words—usually from four to eight words—and absorb them. Then we say them. Then we move on to the next group of words. We look at them, absorb them, and say them. Then we move on to the next group. Every time we move to a new group of words, we have to pause while our eyes focus on them and our brain absorbs them. These are not full stops, but they are noticeable pauses that occur when reading someone else's words and not in extemporaneous speech.

There's no simple trick to solve this problem. You have to train yourself to be looking at the next group of words with your eyes and absorbing them with your brain while your mouth is saying the last group. Your eyes, and your brain, in other words, are always at least one group of words ahead of your mouth. With enough training, they can even be two groups ahead. Training your eyes to stay ahead of your mouth isn't easy. You really have to work at it before it becomes automatic. As the apocryphal little old man said when a stranger on the street asked how to get to Carnegie Hall, "Practice, practice."

As mentioned, when we extemporize, we usually start by taking a big healthy breath. Then we keep talking until we reach the end of a thought. But when we read from a script, there is a tendency to start with less than a full lungful of air. We compound the problem by taking a tiny sip of air each time we pause for our eyes to jump to another group of words. This habit, when we finally start to keep our eyes ahead of our mouth, makes us feel as though we are constantly running out of breath. The out-of-air feeling makes us start to look for more places to stop and take more tiny sips of air, which defeats the whole process.

Understand what happens when you breathe. Carbon dioxide is expelled from your lungs and oxygen is taken in. Note that the carbon dioxide has to get out of your lungs and the oxygen has to get in. To accomplish either of these tasks, you have to take a healthy breath. The gasses have to get all the way out of your lungs and all the way back in. Little sips of air, though, only move a minute volume of air. Some carbon dioxide is expelled, but only that contained in the top few inches of your trachea. And the oxygen you breathe in only fills that same top few inches of the trachea; it never gets down into your lungs. Hence, your lungs deplete more and more of the precious little oxygen they still contain. The oxygen level in your blood drops, the carbon dioxide level rises and, in just eight seconds, the brain, which uses fully 15 percent of the body's blood supply, begins to feel deprived of oxygen. Your medulla oblongata, which controls respiration, among other functions, starts screaming at your autonomic nervous system to make you breathe. As a result, you start looking for even more places to take even more little sips of air and the vicious cycle gets tighter.

To avoid the trap of shallow breathing, you must consciously train yourself to take deep breaths each and every time you breathe while reading. Another trick you can use is to purposely hyperventilate before you start reading. Fill your lungs with as much air as they can hold. Hold it for a slow five count, then exhale, deliberately forcing every possible bit of air out of your lungs. Again, breathe as deeply as you possibly can, holding it for another five count. Then, every bit out again. Repeat three or four times, ending with a full breath before you begin to read. Miraculously, the out-of-breath feeling has disappeared and, so long as you don't backslide into taking only tiny sips of air, it won't return.

This same routine, of taking a series of deep breaths, can also be of great help in relieving pre-audition jitters. In fact, it's good for relieving almost any type of nervousness. Try it; it really works.

Deep breathing, however, has one side effect you should be on guard against. The extra oxygen in your blood stream might result in a tendency to speed up your pace and, unless you deliberately hold back, you'll wind up finishing a sixty second spot in fifty seconds. Remember it can happen and make a conscious effort to counteract it.

There's one other very important technique to help cure choppiness in your copy reading. Like many other techniques to improve copy reading, this one is easy to describe and mighty hard to get in the habit of following. Decide, in advance, where the sense of the copy demands a pause. Mark *every single* place you intend to pause. *Every single one!* Avoid, at all costs, the temptation to ignore commas and periods. Believe that the temptation is quite strong to say to yourself, "I don't really need to mark a pause at every period and comma. I already know to stop when I see one of them." The first of those two sentences is absolutely true. The second is the source of the trouble. Indeed you don't have to mark a pause at every comma and period, because, as we'll discuss further in the next chapter, you don't necessarily *want* to pause at every single comma and period. But unless you do something to distinguish between those you want to pause at and those you intend to ignore, you'll either be pausing where you never intended or relying on "instinct" to tell you what to do—and instinct is about as *un*reliable as you can get. The final part of using marked pauses is probably the hardest of all: training yourself to follow your marks and only pausing where you mark.

Once you have all your pauses marked, go back and carefully examine each one to see if it can possibly be eliminated.

Chances are better than even you'll find some pauses you can do without.

Incidentally, needing to take a breath is never a good reason to pause. Granted, it's impossible to keep talking indefinitely without ever breathing. But, to repeat, simply needing to take a breath is *never* a good enough reason to pause; the reason for the pause must come from the content of the copy. If the pause doesn't make sense from the meaning of the copy, you can't pause. If there's a long convoluted sentence that goes on for several lines, you can't just pause any old place for air. You have to search for the most logical place in terms of the meaning of the copy, and take your pause there.

—— LISTEN TO CUT **13** ON THE INSTRUCTIONAL TAPE.

X – Compound Sentences and Conjunctions

Look at the Merrill Lynch script in the sample copy section. To be technically correct, you would have to say that this spot is composed of two compound sentences and two sentence fragments. But if you think of a "sentence" as a single thought, you'll realize that there are really eight complete sentences in this spot.

1–Today the landscape of investment opportunity spreads far and wide.
2–But there is one place they grow in all varieties.
3–To suit every kind of investor.
4–At Merrill Lynch we've brought together a profusion of financial services.
5–To nurture all kinds of investment needs.

6–And it is the skill and care with which we tend them that makes us what we are.

7–Merrill Lynch.

8–A breed apart.

In normal conversation, we might recast some of these sentences so they can be more clearly understood as separate sentences. Even if we kept the same words, our inflection and cadence would make it clear to a listener that each of the eight sentences was an individual thought.

Many good copywriters realize each thought is, in effect, a separate sentence and, as in the Savarin Decaffeinated spot, they punctuate their copy accordingly. Still, there are plenty of copywriters who, as English majors, had "proper" punctuation drilled into them and are still using it. When you encounter this kind of copy, remember you don't have to follow the written punctuation. Look for the individual thoughts and treat them as individual sentences. As we just explained, you don't have to pause at every period or comma. Similarly, you don't have to pause after every thought. Even if you don't pause, though, you need to do something by way of changing your inflection or your pace or, in some other way, indicate that you are embarking on a new thought.

Usually the clauses of a compound sentence are connected by one of the coordinating conjunctions, the most common of which are **and, but, for,** and **or.** Since we consider each clause of a compound sentence to be a separate sentence in and of itself, what do we do with the conjunction? Well, since the first sentence finishes its thought before the conjunction, we usually consider the second sentence as starting with the conjunction. First sentence: YOU HAVE A RIGHT TO A DELICIOUS CUP OF COFFEE. Second sentence: AND THE RIGHT TO PAY A REASONABLE PRICE FOR IT. If our choice is to indicate the end of the first sentence by a pause, we normally put the pause *before* the conjunction.

There are times, though, when you want to indicate that,

although this thought is finished, there is another closely related one coming up immediately. In such cases, it is permissible to end the first sentence with the conjunction and put the pause after it. YOU HAVE A RIGHT TO A DELICIOUS CUP OF COFFEE AND (pause) THE RIGHT TO PAY A REASONABLE PRICE FOR IT.

So, to sum up what we've said so far: in the case of compound sentences connected by a coordinating conjunction, if you choose to pause, the normal place for the pause is *before* the conjunction, although, in some cases, it may be effective to place the pause *after* the conjunction.

While it is perfectly acceptable to place the pause either before or after the conjunction, it is unacceptable to put a pause in both places. Don't do this:

YOU HAVE A RIGHT TO A DELICIOUS CUP OF COFFEE (pause) AND (pause) THE RIGHT TO PAY A REASONABLE PRICE FOR IT.

One of those pauses is superfluous and makes your reading sound choppy because it is counter to the technique that we've already discussed, eliminating all unnecessary pauses. The rule is: You may pause before a conjunction or you may pause after a conjunction, but you should never pause both before and after a conjunction.

The clauses of compound sentences are sometimes connected by a conjunctive adverb (**however, moreover, whereas, consequently, therefore**) instead of a conjunction. These do not occur frequently in commercial copy, but they are likely to turn up in narrations such as for industrial films. The rule still holds: Before or after but not both.

———— LISTEN TO CUT **14** ON THE INSTRUCTIONAL TAPE.

XI – Adding, Omitting or Changing Words

In a word, don't! By the time a piece of copy reaches your hands, it has been written, rewritten, pored over by a committee, rewritten again, revised by the client, scrutinized by the legal department and, probably, given a final blessing by the agency head himself. Each word has been examined, some have been changed, and the final result is about as close as you'll get in the secular world to the inviolability of sacred scripture. Your job is to read the words exactly as they appear on the paper. You can't add anything; you can't leave anything out; you can't change anything. Just read it, as the old saying goes, "like you sees it."

There are good and sound reasons why you aren't free to alter the copy. Additions and deletions can subtly change the meaning of a sentence. "The best" isn't quite the same thing as "one of the best." Look at the Chevrolet copy. They want you to think the car is being sold at the lowest price they can get away with legally telling you about. Once you get in the salesroom, they're hoping the excitement of seeing a new Cavalier and the persuasiveness of their salesman will overcome the shock when you find out the real bottom-line cost after adding in all the "optional" extras. So they say the car sells for under $7,000. But they can't stop there, or somebody might come in and actually demand to get one at that price. We have to explicitly state that $7,000 is only the sticker price. We can't even stop there, because that's only the *base* sticker price; before they add on all the extras. Anyone who has bought a new car knows the base sticker price is a lot less than the bottom line on the sticker and that bottom line still isn't near what you finally end up paying when you write the check. So the dealer wants to get you into the store by quoting the lowest price he can. Then, when he has you in his clutches, he can start adding a little charge here and a little charge there much like hanging ornaments on a Christmas tree.

But his lawyer makes him put in those extra words and you have *got* to say them.

"Base sticker price" is an example of what are sometimes called "weasel words" because they help weasel past uncomfortable issues. "Use only as directed," "substantial interest penalty for early withdrawal," and "certain restrictions apply, see your travel agent for details" are all examples of weasel words. Another category of weasel words is one that isn't really that bad, but is merely some legal language required by some regulation. "Member FDIC." Either way, the proper method of handling weasel words is to make them as unobtrusive as possible. You have to say them, but you don't have to make a big thing out of them. Use as little emphasis as possible. Make it what actors call a "throw-away line." After all, if you think about a line like "EPA estimate; your mileage may vary" you know full well which way that mileage is going to vary. So you don't want your listener to think about it at all. You say it as quickly and as drably as possible, and then move on to something else that will dazzle him before he's had a chance to think about the weasel words.

Although you have no authority to add, delete or change a single word of the copy, if you think you can back it up with a good reason, you should feel perfectly free to make a suggestion. If, for example, the copy says "it is" and you feel that sounds stilted and formal, go ahead and suggest that "it's" would sound more natural and believable. Sometimes they'll go along with your suggestion; sometimes they won't. Just be sure not to make any changes on your own.

On rare occasions, you'll get a piece of copy that contains a phrase that is an impossible-to-read tongue twister. Practice it. Try your utmost to get through it. If all your efforts have failed and the producer hasn't already thought of rephrasing it, explain your problem and ask politely if there isn't some other way you could say the same thing. It's in their interest to have the spot come out sounding as good as possible, so they'll work with you.

Marking Copy

I – Why Mark Copy?

Think about all the things you have to remember when you're reading a piece of copy. First of all, you need to adopt and hold a tone of delivery consonant with the mood or feeling you're trying to create. You have to mentally picture the person you're speaking to and keep in mind your relationship to that person. You have to remember not to project and not to emphasize personal pronouns. As you read along, you must constantly be alert for new subjects that have to be established and you must remember which subjects have already been established so you don't emphasize them the next time they appear. You must be ever vigilant against the pernicious descending ending. You have to decide where a deliberate up ending would be most effective. You have to recognize when one idea is finished and a new concept is being taken up and you must adjust your reading accordingly. You have to recognize each comparison and contrast and decide which words to stress to bring out that comparison or contrast. Are there any words that would be more effective with word coloring? Don't lose the mood you're trying for. There's a comma; can I pause there? Did I already establish this subject? Here's a non-verbal sound. How do I approach it? Keep picturing your listener. Boy-oh-boy, do I ever need to take a breath! Is this comparison single or a pair? Is this the beginning of a new thought? Timing! I forgot about the timing! Am I going too fast or too slow? Keep that picture of the listener in mind. Talk directly to her. Where can I pause; I've *got* to take a breath! There's a question mark. Does it need an up or down ending? The meaning! Keep trying to convey meaning. Don't project. Keep it conversational. Is this the last time I get to mention the product name, or does the billboard come a line later? OK, I can see the end coming up. Guard against the final ending letdown. Keep it up! The time! Check the stopwatch. Am I going to make it? Warmth! I forgot to smile. Is it too late now, or will it be a nice closing touch? Here comes the big ending! Watch out for the three-word name. Equal stress on each word. Wait! Isn't that a comparison? Keep the listener pictured in your mind. Timing! Warmth! Pauses! Inflection! Comparisons! Coloring! Endings!

Is it humanly possible to keep all these concerns on your mind at the same time and still give a natural and believable reading? Is it even possible to keep all these concerns on your mind at the same time, never mind the naturalness and believability? Of course not! It's worse than the old business of trying to rub your stomach and pat your head simultaneously. In the words of Maria Muldaur's recording "I'm A Woman," you're trying to feed the baby, grease the car and powder your face at the same time. And you simply can't do it. Not if you try to do it all by yourself without any tools or crutches. Fortunately, the best tool you can use, the best crutch you can lean on is also one of the simplest. The simplest and the hardest to do. Mark your copy—and follow your markings!

If you tried to keep everything at a conscious level of awareness, your mind wouldn't be able to do it. The best you could do would be to keep switching your attention from one point to another. Of course, when you prepare the copy—when you analyze it and decide who you'll be talking to and what their relation is to you and what the emotional motivation is, when you study the copy to decide what subjects need to be established and when and where the comparisons and contrasts come and what words need to be colored and where the transitions come and where is a legitimate place to pause—when you decide all these things while preparing the copy, you make a lot of the decisions ahead of time, not while you're actually reading the copy.

But you have to *remember* all this stuff while you are doing the actual reading. And while you're reading, you still have enough to do without trying to remember what decisions you previously made. You have to keep visualizing your listener. You have to keep it conversational. You have to keep the mood or emotional tone you're trying to achieve. And you have to *remember* what decisions you have made and implement these decisions by making your mouth do what your mind and your memory want it to do. It still can't be done. You can't be concentrating on what you're doing while trying to remember what you decided you wanted to do next. Something has to go. Concentrating on what you're doing must remain, so the only thing left to go is relying on your memory.

Now, if you can't rely on your memory, what can you substitute? There's a saying to the effect that the best memory in the world is a pencil and a piece of paper. In the copy, you already have the piece of paper. All you need now is a pencil. Note, the instrument of choice is a *pencil,* not a pen. Pencils allow you to erase and change your markings; pens lock you into your first interpretation. Like the person who does a crossword puzzle with a pen, the performer who marks copy in ink is running a real risk of, as he works on a piece of copy, finding the first choice wasn't the right choice after all. The only way to change things, then, is to scribble over one set of markings and put in some others. Confusing, at best, when you're trying to read it! Then, what do you do when you find your second choice wasn't the best, either?

Save yourself a lot of grief: *never, ever* mark copy in ink; *always, always* do your copy marking in pencil. And be sure your pencil has a nice, big eraser on the end of it. You can be certain you'll need it.

"Oh, come on, now!" you might say. "Isn't all of this pretty much like what the Bible calls 'straining at a gnat'? Why can't a person simply go ahead and read the copy? After all, English is our native language. Can't we just rely on our instinct to guide us to the proper way to read the copy?" It's a tempting idea but, unfortunately, it doesn't work out that way in practice. Our "instinct" works in different ways depending on the circumstances. If we are extemporizing, our instinct unerringly tells us what to do, because our sole concern is expressing the idea we have in mind. But with copy, we're stuck with someone else's words. We have to go through the tortuous process of figuring out what the original ideas were behind the copy. We can't rely on our instinct because our instinct, when confronted with a page of printed words, is to just read the words. What else can we expect of our instinct? That is, after all, what we've been doing all our lives! Or, alternatively—since we subconsciously know we are "announcing"—our instinct leads us to imitate what we think an "announcer" would sound like, and we fall into the trap of the small-station lilt.

Clearly, then, we can't rely on our instinct to tell us what to do when we are trying to convey meaning to our listener and we have to get that meaning, for ourselves, from someone else's words. We have to make deliberate, rational choices based, not on what "feels right," nor what you think "sounds right" at the moment, but, rather, on what careful study reveals to us about the original intent of the person or persons who wrote the copy. All our lives, we have approached the written word and the extemporaneously spoken word differently. Now, we have to abandon all those old habits and retrain ourselves to make rational choices, mark our copy to remind ourselves of those choices and follow those markings totally and completely.

Yet another reason to mark your copy, to follow the

markings and to change the markings when you find a better choice, is the fallibility of memory, not only in regard to remembering what you intended to do, but, also, in regard to what you have already done. It is not unknown for a producer to say to a performer, during a recording session, something like "The way you said 'sweet and delicious' that time was just perfect. That's exactly right; keep it." You stand there and wonder, "What in the world did I just do? This is the fifteenth take and I have no idea what was different from the other takes." If you had conscientiously marked your copy and changed the markings each time you decided on a better reading—and *followed* your markings—there would be no question. Otherwise, you have to go through the embarrassing business of asking them for a replay on the last take so that you can hear what it is that you did. A professional will *know* exactly what he has done and be able to duplicate it on command.

II—How We Mark Copy

There is no such thing as a standard system of copy marking. People develop their own systems depending upon what they most need to remind themselves of. Following are some of the most common items that require marking, and *one*—but certainly not the only—way of marking copy. The copy markings suggested in this section are just that: suggestions. Some of them are the author's own inventions, some have been suggested by students and some have been adapted from other sources. Nobody ever went to the top of a mountain and came down with a tablet inscribed with the one and only set of copy markings you should use. Each person encounters different problems in reading copy and whatever markings you choose to use should be a help to you in coping with those problems. It isn't so important what kind of a system you use. What is important is that you do develop your own copy marking system and that you use it.

Stress

The most important thing to decide when preparing to read a piece of copy is which words you will stress and which words you will not. We've already discussed the techniques for making such decisions: establishing the subject, identifying comparisons and contrasts, and looking for words to be reestablished in the closing billboards. Once these decisions have been made, it's necessary to mark the words we intend to stress so that we don't have to do it all by memory. The most common way to mark for stress is to underline the word.

LET'S TALK ABOUT A COUPLE OF <u>NUMBER ONES</u>.

Since underlining is the most common marking for stress, and since the most common way to stress a word is to "punch" it (say it louder), it follows that an underlined word is usually stressed by punching it.

In Chapter 4, you learned a number of ways to emphasize a word besides punching it. If you intend to say a word more softly, you might write above it "wh" for "whisper" or "so" for "softly." If you want to remember to say a particular word more quickly, the letter "Q" written above the word will work nicely. To remind yourself to say a word more slowly, try "sl" or "st" for "stretch." If you intend to use word coloring a notation might be "clr" or, simply circle the word. A circle around a word can also alert you to the need for a nonverbal sound.

Inflection

There are only three things you can do with inflection: you can go up, go down or stay at the same level. A small arrow pointing in the appropriate direction should be more than sufficient.

HE'S GOT THE <u>NUMBER</u> <u>ONE</u> SELLING CAR IN ↗

<u>AMERICA</u>—THE <u>CHEVY</u> <u>CAVALIER.</u> ↘ →

Pauses

In the last chapter, we talked about the problem of choppiness. We recommended that to cure choppiness, you should develop the habit of marking each and every pause in the copy, and then, train yourself to pause only at those points where you have marked a pause. But all pauses are not alike. There's the full pause that comes after the completion of a thought. You might want to indicate such a full pause with a vertical line (|). These are the pauses at which you can take a breath. When you finish a complete concept and are moving on to another one, you might want to use the proofreader's mark for a new paragraph (¶). For a short pause, a diagonal slash (/) serves well, and when you want to indicate just the slightest hesitation, try using an asterisk (*). When, on the other hand, you want to indicate to yourself that you should *not* pause, try using what, in music, is called a slur: a curved line connecting one word to another (⌢).

LET'S TALK ABOUT A COUPLE OF NUM-

BER ONES./YOU AND YOUR TRI-STATE

CHEVROLET DEALER. | YOU, BECAUSE

YOU'RE LOOKING OUT FOR NUMBER ONE AND WANT A REAL VALUE ON A QUALITY NEW CAR.* YOUR TRI-STATE CHEVY DEALER BECAUSE HE'S GOT THE NUMBER ONE SELLING CAR IN AMERICA.// THE CHEVY CAVALIER. ¶ AS A MATTER OF FACT, YOUR TRI-STATE CHEVY DEALER HAS SIX DIFFERENT CAVALIER MODELS / BASE STICKER PRICED UNDER SEVEN THOUSAND DOL-LARS. ¶ SO LOOK OUT FOR NUMBER ONE. / LOOK FOR THE NUMBER ONE SELLING CAVALIER. / LOOK TO YOUR TRI-STATE CHEVY DEALER.

Remember, these are only suggestions. Some of these markings will be of help to you while some may not. You don't have to use each and every one of them in exactly the same way as shown here. Feel free to change them. Make up totally new ones. Experiment and find out what works best for you. If you are using this text in conjunction with a formal class, your teacher may want to see how you mark your copy and may make some

suggestions as to how you can improve your markings. But remember, markings are only a means to an end. They should help
you improve your reading; help you sound more natural and believable. Copy marking is never an end in itself. Nobody in the
real world is going to be looking over your shoulder to see how
you mark your copy. The only important thing to them is how the
finished product sounds coming out of the speaker.

Timing

Radio and television stations make their money from sponsors
and the sponsors' advertising agencies. The sponsors want to
reach an audience with a commercial message about their product. Like other merchants, stations sell their product in units of
specific quantity. Milk comes in pints, quarts, and gallons. Flour
and sugar come by the pound. Electricity is sold by the kilowatt-
hour. Taxicab rides are priced by the mile or fraction of a mile.
Broadcast time is sold in quantities of ten, twenty, thirty, and sixty
seconds. When a spot is written, it is designed to fill the allotted
time. Sometimes, though, the copywriter's idea of what will fill
the time may be quite different from yours. Some copy can be
read at a very leisurely pace and you'll still have time to spare.
Other times, you'll have to read as fast as you possibly can and
you'll still barely come in under the wire. So the first thing you
want to do after analyzing a piece of copy is to read it through
aloud, to see whether your normal pace is sufficient or whether
you'll need to speed up or stretch.

      It is important when you read for timing to read aloud.
Granted, it may be a little embarrassing in some circumstances to
really read aloud, but at least be sure that you move your lips as
you read. This may go contrary to years of conditioning in which
you were led to believe only dimwitted or semiliterate persons
move their lips as they read. But that stereotype stems from the
fact that, for most people, the eye can scan and the brain can absorb at a greater rate than the lips can speak. So, when you read

silently, you will cover more material than you would if reading aloud. Therefore, a silent reading is of no value whatsoever in timing copy. The only way to get an accurate timing is to read aloud.

Some ten or fifteen years ago, there was a short-lived* fad involving bumper stickers and wall signs that looked like this:

```
┌─────────────────────────┐
│                         │
│   PLAN AHEAD            │
│                         │
└─────────────────────────┘
```

Something similar to this predicament is experienced by the person who takes a leisurely pace while reading a one minute spot and discovers, at the fifty-five-second point, that they still have at least ten more seconds of copy to cover. Months or years later, the results may be recalled with humor. But at the time, you can rest assured you won't think it's one bit funny.

Avoiding this problem is as simple as the motto in the sign above: plan ahead. If you have a sixty second spot, make a mark in the margin halfway through. Make two other marks, one of them a fourth of the way into the copy and another at the three-quarter point. While reading, use these marks to pace yourself. When you reach the first mark, glance quickly at the stopwatch. If, suppose, it says seventeen seconds, you know you've been going a trifle too slow. Pick up the pace just a little. When you reach the second mark, check the stopwatch again. Now you find you're exactly on time. Great! At the third mark, you see that it's only forty-three seconds into the spot. You know you can relax just a bit and still bring it home on time.

---

* Incidentally, the word "lived" in "short-lived" should be pronounced so it rhymes with "pie" or "sky"—not with "give."

With a thirty second spot, you'll only need two marks: at ten seconds and at twenty. For a twenty second spot, one mark—at the halfway point—is sufficient.

Mark EVERYTHING

One of the main theses of this text has been that, when reading aloud, most people habitually do certain things that make them sound different from when they speak extemporaneously and, in order to properly do voice-overs, you must become aware of these habits and eliminate them. Doing so, however, is quite difficult. First of all, we are rarely even conscious of doing things that have become habitual. And that's the way it should be; we'd be unable to function at all if we had to give conscious thought to all the things, from the simple to the complex, that we do in daily life. Walking down a flight of stairs, using a knife and fork to cut meat, using a typewriter, driving a car, even pouring and drinking a glass of milk. Think of how long it takes before a young child is able to perform that simple task for himself. First, he must build up an entire repertory of habits that, when combined, allow the hand-eye coordination necessary to pick up the milk carton, pour from it, return it to the refrigerator, pick up the glass, put it to his lips and drink. He never thinks about the mechanics of what he is doing, only the end he's striving for.

Since habits are, by their very nature, things that we do without thinking about them, we have to do something to bring an undesirable habit to our conscious attention before we can break it. One way to do this when reading copy is to carefully and completely mark your copy, and then to train yourself to follow your markings religiously. The second part of this prescription is a lot more difficult than the first because, even with the most dedicated effort, you'll find the old habits creeping in without your having realized it. So listen carefully to your practice recordings, paying specific attention to whether you have accurately followed your markings. You'll be surprised how often you drop back to an undesirable habit without being aware of it.

One of the things most people do when reading aloud is to slavishly follow the punctuation as written on the page. We have already seen, however, that the rules of written grammar aren't much help when striving for a pseudo-conversational style; they may, in fact, be detrimental. So we have to consciously break the habit of following the written punctuation. No longer do we want to pause every time we see a comma. No longer do we want to automatically use a down inflection every time we see a period and an up inflection whenever we encounter a question mark. The ellipsis, those ubiquitous three little dots, is now to be ignored.

Still, without some sort of written guide as an integral part of the copy, we're heading for verbal chaos. Hence, the need for substituting our own markings for the ones we intend to ignore. The problem is compounded by the fact that many, if not most, of the original punctuation marks will be accurate and fine to follow. We don't want to go counter to every single mark of written punctuation. We only want to break the habit of blindly following punctuation without any regard to the meaning we're supposed to be trying to convey. Yet, like the cigarette smoker who tries to quit smoking by gradually cutting down, we find that if we only mark some things and let ourselves rely on the original punctuation for others, we will inevitably backslide and find ourselves unconsciously following the original punctuation even when we didn't intend to—just as the smoker, without actually realizing it, suddenly finds himself back at his old level of cigarette consumption. If you're going to break a habit, you've got to break it totally. Therefore, even if the original punctuation is quite appropriate to spoken language—even if you really want to pause at a particular comma, even if you fully intend to use an up inflection at a particular question mark—put your own markings on the copy so that you will be following only your markings, and can break the habit of following the original punctuation. As time goes by and you gradually develop new habits to replace the old ones, you'll find that you'll need to mark less on your copy. But at this beginning stage, NEVER RELY ON THE PUNCTUATION THAT'S ALREADY THERE; ALWAYS MARK EVERYTHING!

Before you continue, practice what you have already learned. Turn to the script section in the back of this book and look at the spot for Delta Airlines. Analyze it by writing out your answers to the four basic questions:

1. To whom are you speaking?
2. What is your relationship to the listener?
3. What is your relationship to the product?
4. What is the motivator?

Now, go back and reread the section of Chapter 3 dealing with these questions. If you need to revise your answers, do so. Mark your copy and practice recording the spot. Listen to each attempt and revise your copy markings as necessary. When you are satisfied with your recording, let your instructor (if you are in a formal class) or members of your study group listen to it. Also let them see your analysis of the basic questions and your marked copy.

Once you have had the advantage of feedback from your instructor or your fellow students on the Delta spot, turn to the spot for G.T.E. Growlux. Go through the same process: analyze the four basic questions, mark the copy, practice and revise as necessary and, finally, get feedback from your instructor or fellow students. Do the same for the Bank of New York spot.

Demo Reels

I – Preparation

A common sight on buses and subway cars in Manhattan and, to a lesser extent, in some other major cities, is a tall, slender, beautiful young woman carrying a large, thin, black leather case. The woman is a model and the case is her portfolio which contains pictures of her in a variety of locations and costumes. In one shot, she'll be wearing a fancy ball gown; in another, sports clothes, and in yet another, a bathing suit. The backgrounds will vary as well: Lincoln Center or Carnegie Hall, a modern kitchen, the racetrack, a farm or country estate. The model's portfolio serves two related purposes: it demonstrates that she photographs exceptionally well, and secondly, it shows that she is able to look attractive and natural in a variety of settings and styles of clothing. When a model calls on an agent or casting director, she presents her portfolio to show how versatile she is and how she might appear were she to be used in a billboard, magazine ad or other photographic depiction on behalf of a particular product. In many cases, a model may be chosen without the casting director ever having met him or her. Selection is done on the basis of the model's portfolio or, in some cases, a composite. The composite is a piece of paper, usually printed on both sides, with a collection of photographs that, like the more elaborate portfolio, shows the model in a variety of costumes and settings. Some people who have extremely attractive personalities, when photographed appear quite ordinary, or even somewhat unattractive. Conversely, some people who are, frankly, quite blah in person photograph as highly attractive. Agents and casting directors, therefore, pay little attention to the personality of the model when they see her in person; they are only concerned with the way the model looks in the portfolio or composite.

Similarly, a voice-over performer can't rely on her total personality to get her the job. A handsome or beautiful face, perfect posture, a well-endowed body, graceful movements—all are irrelevant. The only thing that matters is how you sound. The casting director knows no one will see you; they will only hear you. So the only thing that is assessed when you are considered for a voice-over job is how you *sound*. The way you demonstrate how you sound—the aural equivalent of the model's portfolio or composite—is your demonstration tape.

Most often referred to as your *demo reel*, a demonstration tape is a magnetic tape recording of your interpretation of several kinds of copy for several kinds of products. It shows the agent or casting director what you can do.

Agents and casting directors are in business to provide talent for commercials. When a producer needs a performer with certain qualities, it is up to the casting director and, subsequently, the agents called by the casting director, to come up with a number of people who meet the producer's specifications. The more people they can produce and the closer the candidates meet the specifications, the better the agent or casting director's reputation. They are judged by the number and quality of the talent they provide. As such, agents and casting directors are always alert to find new and marketable talent.

Yet their quest presents a dilemma: there are far more

people anxious to break into the business than anyone can possibly interview. Only a small fraction of these hopefuls, however, have the talent, training and experience to make them truly marketable. Obviously, some sort of screening process is necessary, and that's where your demo reel comes in. An in-person interview will probably take an average of fifteen minutes. Listening to a demo reel takes much less time. Assuming the reel runs two minutes, and allowing for another two minutes to thread the reel on the machine and rewind after listening, it will come to somewhere near four minutes per reel. In a four hour afternoon, an agent can either meet with fifteen potential performers in person or, in the same amount of time, listen to sixty demo tapes. Which is the most efficient use of the agent's time? Plainly, it's going to be much easier to get an agent or casting director to listen to your demo tape than to interview you in person. Even ignoring the advantage of time efficiency, as we've already explained, how you present yourself in an in-person interview bears little if any relationship to how you perform in a voice-over, where the only thing going for you is what you can do with your voice.

Obviously, then, your demo tape is the *sine qua non* for your career as a voice-over performer. It's the way you get in the door. And the next door. And the next. But only if it is a good tape. Only if it presents you favorably. Only if it convinces the agent or casting director listening to it that you are a marketable commodity.

How, then, do you insure that your demo tape presents you as well as possible? First, your demo tape should be an accurate representation of your particular vocal personality. It should also demonstrate your versatility, and finally, it should be enhanced with appropriate production.

Your Vocal Personality

Each person's sound is distinctive. The characteristics that account for vocal uniqueness are numerous, and include the natural pitch, the number and characteristics of the overtones, the way the speaker chooses to inflect various words, the frequency of pauses and where they are inserted, the energy level, the speed of delivery and level of warmth—to name only a few items. Some vocal personalities are quite versatile while others are limited in the range of spots that they can believably deliver. Take Mason Adams, for example. An accomplished actor, Adams began his career in the forties as the title role on a radio soap opera called "Pepper Young's Family." Most notably, he has played the role of editor Charlie Hume on the television series "Lou Grant." Later he was teamed with Jack Warden in the TV sitcom, "Night and Day." Although he has done countless voice-overs in his career, Adams is best known for his spots on behalf of a California company that produces jams, jellies and preserves. Adams' voice has become inextricably linked with the phrase "with a name like Smuckers, it's *got* to be good." Adams' vocal personality is gentle and friendly. He can be serious or frivolous, but there is always a neighborliness in his sound that comes through loud and clear. He definitely sounds kindly; that is his vocal personality.

A different vocal personality is presented by Ernie Anderson. As the voice-over for ABC television prime-time programs, Anderson is probably best known for his promotional spots for the program "The Love Boat." Anderson has a hard-hitting style that comes across as very forceful and dynamic. When, on commercials for automobiles, he tells us that "Dodge trucks are ram-tough," you tend to believe him because he sounds so tough himself.

Anderson wouldn't sound nearly as appropriate as Adams were he to do the Smuckers spots. And Adams wouldn't be nearly as good a choice to voice the Dodge spot. Everyone has her own vocal personality, and certain types of spots are better suited to that personality than others. The only way to determine your own vocal personality is to purposely try as many different kinds of copy as you can find. After a while, you'll begin to develop a "feel" for the kinds of spots you do best. Listening to playbacks of your own work, you'll start to discern a pattern: certain kinds of spots will sound right while others won't.

—— LISTEN TO CUT **15** ON THE INSTRUCTIONAL TAPE.

What Copy to Use

Once you have a firm idea of what kinds of spots work best with your vocal personality, you can start to plan your demo reel. Whatever your vocal personality, there will be a range of copy you can do well, and within that range, you should select as wide a variety of copy styles as you can. The whole idea of putting several spots on the reel is to show your versatility. It would be of little value for you to make a demo reel with nothing but spots for automobiles, all delivered with a lot of energy and excitement. Agents and casting directors are quite busy and won't waste their time listening to your entire tape unless it is constantly showing them something new. Once they've heard how you approach, say, a lighthearted humorous spot, their attitude is "Fine. I know you can do that kind of copy. Now show me something different." The next spot should not be another humorous one. It might be a serious, businesslike spot, for a bank, perhaps. That could be followed by a perfume spot delivered in a soft, seductive tone and, for the final spot, you might try a hard-sell punch-type spot.

The first spot on the tape has to capture and hold the listener's attention, so start out with what you feel is your best spot. The next spot should be as great a contrast as possible to the first one. The third should have an entirely different approach from the second and the fourth should be a change from the third. Each spot should lead directly into the next with no or only the slightest of pauses. Of course, it should not sound as though all your spots are one long, single spot. But if you have chosen spots of sufficiently diverse character, and if you have varied your approach, this will not be a problem. Should it happen, even with different copy styles and diverse approaches in your delivery, that the transition from one spot to another isn't clear, you can insert a fraction of a second of blank tape between the two spots. Be very careful, though, that it is indeed only a fraction of a second, because if the pause is too long, the listener may decide the tape is finished. Excessively long pauses present a real danger of the listener turning off the machine and never hearing the rest of your tape.

As we mentioned, agents and casting directors are busy people. In their careers, they listen to hundreds, if not thousands, of demo tapes. They know exactly what to listen for and can evaluate your work very quickly. So keep the length of your spots short, certainly no longer than thirty seconds each. A good agent doesn't even need that much time to know what you are capable of. A spot lasting a full minute is an open invitation to the listener to hit the fast-forward button on their tape recorder. If they do, they may very well go too far and miss some of your best work.

Where Does the Copy Come from?

Finding commercials to include on your demo tape takes a little work, but it's so important to have the right spots that it's well worth the effort. Radio stations are an obvious source. Simply start a tape recorder when you hear a record ending. Let it run until the next record starts. If, during that time, you heard a spot you think might be a good one for your demo reel, take the tape recorder to your typewriter. Rewind the tape, and while listening to the playback, type out the script. If you didn't hear anything you wanted to save, rewind the tape and simply record over it when the next commercial break occurs.

Much the same procedure can be followed to find spots from television. The only difference with TV spots is that you watch for a program or program segment to end.

If you happen to be fortunate enough to work at a radio or TV station or at an advertising agency, raid the company's copy file and head for the photocopy machine. Even if you don't have a job that affords you access to copy, perhaps one of your friends does. Go through your address book and see who might be able to help you find copy.

Each year, a book is published containing the best advertising from a variety of media: magazines, billboards, television and, on occasion, radio. At different times, this annual publication has been put out under different names: *The Art Directors Annual* and *The One Club*. Many public libraries have collected these yearly volumes. Art departments of the larger advertising agencies frequently have these books as well.

A final source for commercials to use on your demo tape is to write your own. This can work quite well if you have had training and experience in writing copy. If, however, you aren't an accomplished copywriter, it may be best to stick to professionally written spots instead of your own home-brewed versions.

Some people will try to use advertisements from newspapers or magazines for their demo tape. In almost every case, the results will be poor because, as we've stressed elsewhere in this book, there is a vast difference between copy written to be read with the eyes and copy written to be heard by the ear. Ads from print media are written to be read by the eye and invariably need extensive rewriting before they are acceptable for use on a demo tape. Again, if you are an accomplished copywriter you might be able to use such print ads as fact-sheets from which you can extract the product information needed to write a good voice-over script. If you don't have such experience, it's a good idea to leave print advertisements alone. Your tape will only be the better for it.

Quality of Spots

Most advertising agencies have at least one full-time copywriter on their staff. Copywriters are specially trained and spend their entire working day producing the best quality scripts they are capable of. Their work is then subjected to review by a number of others in the agency. A good agency can't afford to risk its reputation by putting out shoddy, third-rate work.

Not all commercials you hear, however, are written by agencies. Many stations will, for small clients who can't afford the services of a big advertising agency, provide the copy at no or only a nominal charge. Very large stations in major markets might have someone whose primary duty is to write copy for the station's clients. In most cases, though, it falls under the heading of an "additional" duty. As such, copywriting usually doesn't carry a very high priority. The program director or one of the disc jockeys may get stuck with the job during his off-air hours. Sometimes it's the person who types the logs and answers the telephones. At some stations the salespersons are expected to write the copy for their own clients. Some stations subscribe to services that provide books full of sample copy for every conceivable product or service. The station has only to look up the product in the index, pull out the copy for that kind of product and retype the spot inserting the local client's name in each of the blanks. Some local merchants insist on writing their own spots. Considering all these factors, it isn't too surprising that the quality of locally written and produced advertising on radio and television frequently leaves much to be desired.

Since your demo reel will be your calling card to gain entree to agents and casting directors, you want it to be of the highest quality possible, and that means you want to avoid locally written spots. The easiest way to avoid them is to simply reject any spot for clients of a strictly local nature. With commercials for automobiles, for example, the spots that talk about the technical excellence of the new Chrysler cars consistently display better writing than the spots that tell you what a great deal you can get from Crazy Sam, the Used Car Man; "he's way overstocked and has to move them all off the lot by midnight!"

Even with large chain stores—especially supermarkets —beware of less than desirable writing. The client may not be strictly local, but you will find copy consisting of nothing more than a recitation of products and prices. It gives you nothing to work with, nothing that will show off your skill in voice-overs. And it will bore your listener to tears.

There are several dangers to be aware of when taking spots from TV. A well-written television commercial will frequently interweave the picture with the words in such a way that one reinforces the other, yet neither will stand alone. Remember that the person who will be listening to your tape won't have any picture to look at. All he'll have is your words. If the spot doesn't make sense when he hears it, you're in trouble. If he has to stop listening to how you're handling the copy, and instead divert his attention to trying to figure out what the spot is all about, he will be unable to form an accurate opinion of your work. For the same reason, you don't want to use any spots where you, as the speaker, are obviously on camera. After all, using a line like "see how soft and shiny my hair looks" won't make much sense if the listener can't see anything of the sort. It is important to remember that this is a demo for voice-overs, not on-camera work.

You may have noticed that voice-overs on television commercials frequently take a long pause while something goes on in the picture. With such commercials on your demo reel, it's important to eliminate these pauses. Since your listener doesn't have any picture to watch, the pause comes out sounding like a big, dumb hole right in the middle of the spot. An exception might be a situation where you say a line like, "watch what happens when the active ingredients in Rolaids are added to this concentrated stomach acid." Obviously, a demonstration is supposed to be going on at this point. A pause would be quite appropriate here. You can't, however, just leave silence during the pause. If, on the other hand, the listener hears the plop of a tablet dropping into liquid followed by a fizzing sound, it fills the void and enhances the spot by helping the listener to mentally visualize the video portion.

There is an unspoken agreement between the agents and casting directors who will be listening to your tape, and you.

They know you are just breaking into the business. They realize it's highly unlikely you have already done spots for such important national accounts as Lincoln Town Cars, Bank of America, Obsession perfume and Post Raisin Bran. Yet there they are on your demo tape, all well-produced and sounding as professional as can be. Any agent who's been in the business for more than a day or two knows full well you didn't actually do those spots for those accounts. But no one will ever call you on it. Nobody is going to say "Now, wait a minute. You didn't really do that spot for that sponsor, did you? This is just a big sham, isn't it?"

What's going on here? Why is it you aren't in danger of being denounced as a fraud and a humbug? The answer is in the nature of that tacit agreement between you and your listener. Walt Disney used to call the phenomenon "the willing suspension of disbelief." If actually put into words, the agreement might be phrased this way. AGENT: "Look, we both know you didn't actually do these spots, right?" YOU: "Oh, sure. Of course I didn't. But if I had, this is what I would have sounded like. And it can show you how I'd approach any similar spot that you can set me up to audition for." AGENT: "OK, sounds reasonable. So we'll just pretend that you really did these spots and got paid for them and they aired all over the country. Deep in my heart I know it isn't true, but what the heck! It'll at least give me some idea of how you sound doing these kinds of spots."

One thing that can interfere with this willing suspension of disbelief is to choose a spot that is so well known that there is no way for the listener to pretend you were the one who really did it. Mason Adams is so well known as the voice-over for Smuckers jams and jellies that no matter how well you do the spot, the listener will still be hearing the way Adams does it. Unconsciously, they will be comparing you with Adams. And there is no way that you can come out ahead in such a comparison. The wisest choice, then, is to avoid any spot for your demo reel that is so well known that it has become completely associated with the vocal personality of the person voicing the spot.

PSAs and Promos

Radio and television stations are licensed by the Federal Communications Commission "to operate in the public interest, convenience and necessity."* This is the way Congress expressed the concept that broadcasters are public trustees who don't actually own the airwaves over which they operate; the broadcast spectrum, says Congress, is a public resource which the broadcasters use with the government's permission, much the same way logging companies are permitted to cut timber on public lands. And, also in similar ways, restrictions are put on broadcasters and concessions extracted from them. In return for the privilege of using the publicly owned airwaves, broadcasters assume certain obligations. One of the ways they fulfill these obligations is by airing free commercials for charitable organizations, governmental agencies and other causes in the public interest. The generic name for these commercials is *public service announcement*, usually abbreviated *PSA*. Spots for such diverse topics as the Red Cross Blood Program, foreign food relief funds, the local community theatre group's latest production and antismoking messages all come under the umbrella of PSAs. Although we usually think only of commercials (that is, spots for commercial enterprises) as material for a demo tape, it is perfectly acceptable to include one or more PSAs, so long as they meet the same criteria used for any spot: well-written, no longer than thirty seconds, and, if more than one, a variety of subjects.

In addition to commercial announcements and PSAs, there is one other category of spot announcement you might consider for your demo tape: *promotional announcements* or, more informally, *promos*. As the name suggests, this category of spot promotes something; specifically, the station itself, its activities and its programs.

---

* Communications Act of 1934.

The most common kind of promo is for a particular program. "THIS WEEK, A SPECIAL ENCORE PRESENTATION OF THE MOST HIGHLY ACCLAIMED SHOW OF ALL TIME: 'ROOTS.' " But promos can be about the station in general: "ACCORDING TO THE LATEST LISTENER SURVEYS, YOU'RE LISTENING TO THE NUMBER ONE RADIO STATION IN THE ENTIRE METROPOLITAN WASHINGTON AREA. FOR THREE YEARS IN A ROW, NOW, WE CAME OUT ON TOP! AND WE WANT TO THANK YOU, OUR LISTENERS, FOR MAKING IT HAPPEN AGAIN." Promos can also be for one of the station's activities: "TONIGHT, WE'LL BE BROADCASTING DIRECTLY FROM THE NEW TOWER RECORDS STORE ON SIXTY-SIXTH STREET. COME BY, HAVE A FREE CUP OF COFFEE, MEET THE QXR GOOD GUYS AND REGISTER FOR A FREE RECORD ALBUM OF YOUR CHOICE AND A 96.3 T-SHIRT!" There's nothing wrong with including a promo on your demo tape, and it may add variety to your selection of spots. Nevertheless, a promo, like any other spot, should be well written and short.

How Many Spots?

In planning a demo tape, a decision has to be made as to how many different spots to include. The easiest answer is another question: how many different kinds of copy can you do well? Most people are capable of at least three of four different approaches and a tape with less than three spots would fail to show all their skills. The maximum number of spots is determined by how many different approaches you can take without appearing repetitive. For many, that upper limit will probably be five or six.

Character Voices

Some people feel they have a talent for character or "gimmick" voices—regional or ethnic dialects, sounding like an octagenarian, a little child or an adolescent. If you are really good at character voices—IF YOU ARE *REALLY* GOOD—you might stand a slight chance of success in this field. But understand that as competitive as regular voice-over work may be, the field of character voices is even more tightly-knit and hard to break into. The reasons are twofold: First, there simply isn't that much work for character voices. The vast majority of the work in voice-overs calls for "straight" voices. You can prove it to yourself: sit down to watch television tonight with a pad and pencil. Keep track of how many spots use straight voices in their voice-overs and how many, if any, use character voice-overs. The defense rests! Of course, there are some small number of spots using character voices. To get one of those jobs, however, you'll have to go up against the likes of Stan Freberg, Bert Burtis, Dick Orken, June Foray, Jesse White, Jack Mercer, Allan Melvin, Arnold Stang, or Herb Hartig. That's just a random sampling of names. There are more, and each is an accomplished and experienced performer. This is the second reason the field of character voice-overs is so difficult to break into: there are many professionals in the field who have been doing character voices for years. Most of them got into the field because they were already successful actors and actresses. To put it succinctly, they are very, very good at what they do. So good, in fact, that your chances of breaking into the charmed circle of successful character-voice performers is quite slim.

If, despite the gloomy outlook, you still want to take a crack at doing character voices, here's one way to approach your quest more professionally: don't put any character voices on your straight voice-over demo. Instead, make a separate tape for your character voices. The reason for this advice is the way voice-overs are cast. Most agents and casting directors keep straight demo tapes apart from character tapes, either on different shelves or, in some cases, even in different offices. When looking for people to audition for a character voice, no one would think of going to their collection of straight demos. Conversely, it makes little sense to listen to a lot of character tapes when you're looking for a straight voice. Remember, these are busy people and they'll invariably take the quickest, most efficient approach. So play the game their way. If you really believe you have a chance to make it as a character voice, don't waste your listener's time by putting both straight and character voices on the same tape. Instead, make two different tapes; label one "Ned Newguy, Voice-Over Demo" and the other "Ned Newguy, Character Voice Demo." Of course, the same rules for copy selection apply to character voice demos as do to straight tapes. Get well-written spots, a good variety of products and approaches, and keep them short.

Finding Copy for Your Own Tape

At this point, you should start work on your own demo tape. Before you read any farther, you need to find some spots (or PSAs or promos) you could use on your own tape. First, review the procedure for recording spots off radio and television outlined in the beginning of this chapter. Next, sit down with your tape recorder and a radio. Spend a few hours trying to find spots you think might be good for your particular vocal personality. Remember to strive for as wide a variety of products and approaches as possible. To that end, you may find it helpful to listen to stations with differing formats and at different times of day. Keep at it until you have four to six spots you feel would be appropriate for your tape.

    a) Analyze the spots by answering the four basic
       questions.
    b) Mark the copy.
    c) Practice the spots, listening to each attempt and re-
       vising your markings as necessary.

d) When you are thoroughly satisfied, record the
   spots and get feedback from your instructor or
   study group.

By now, you should be confident enough in your craft to
understand what does and doesn't work well for you. Feedback
from others can be helpful, but only you can make the final decision about what is and isn't right for your tape. Should you find
the insight gained from your instructor and friends helpful, go
ahead and rework the spots incorporating the suggestions you've
received.

The next task is to find four to six spots from *television*.
Again, look for spots you feel would be best for your vocal style,
while seeking as wide a range of products and approaches as possible. As with radio, it may be helpful to watch several stations at
different times of day. Once you are satisfied with your selection
of spots, follow steps a) through d) above.

Finally, explore any additional source you might have
other than radio or television. The important thing here is for you
to find spots you have never heard being done by someone else.
As usual, try to find as wide a variety of products as possible.
Since you won't be influenced by hearing someone else's style,
you will have to decide for yourself the proper way to approach
these spots. They will probably be your best voice-overs because
they will be completely your own. Follow steps a) through d).

Once you have assembled the possible candidates for
your demo tape, you will have to make a tentative decision as to
which spots to discard and which to keep. When you finally decide on the four spots you will use, you have to decide the order
in which you will use them. Try for as much contrast as possible
between spots. You don't want all hard sell or all soft sell, or all
formal or all informal, or all of anything. The best selection will
present one of each kind of spot you are capable of doing well.
Test out the order you've chosen by making a "first draft" of your
demo tape. Record the spots in the order you've decided upon.
Don't put anything between them; leave as little space as possible

from spot to spot. When you listen to the result, pay attention to how one spot relates to another and what impression the tape creates as a whole. Get feedback from your instructor or study group.

Finding Production for Your Own Tape

After you have listened to the comments of your instructor or study group on the first draft of your demo tape, decide what changes you would like to make in the spots themselves or the order in which they appear. Then it's time to decide what production to use for each spot. Of course, it isn't necessary to have production for each and every spot. Some spots are of such a formal or serious nature they may be better left standing without any production at all.

Production Material

Since your demo reel, ostensibly, contains spots you at least *could* have really done, you'll want them to sound as professional as possible. That means you'll want to use some music and/or sound effects on at least some of your spots. Both music and sound effects fall into the generic category of *production material* and the process of adding them to a tape is called *production*. Done properly and judiciously, production can do a lot to enhance your voice-over demo reel. The key word in the previous sentence is "enhance." The only reason to ever use production on a spot is to intensify the mood or feeling you want to create; to enhance your performance, never to outshine it. It will do you no good if, after listening to your tape, an agent says, "Wow! What great production!" "Yes," you reply, "but what about the performer's delivery?" "Oh, yeah," the agent answers, "it was all right, I guess, but gee! Wasn't that some dynamite production?" Like that old nuisance, vampire audio, production that is too obtrusive can distract the listener's attention from your performance. If it doesn't convince the listener you are a good voice-over performer, a demo tape is quite useless.

Some spots can stand alone without any kind of production. Others only need a minimum of sound effects to create their mood. A public service announcement about hunger in Africa might be most effective if delivered in a quiet, serious, concerned-sounding voice without any production at all. A few pages back, we gave an example of effective use of sound effects. Remember, it's important to prepare the listener for what she's going to hear. A few words may be sufficient: "watch what happens when the active ingredients in Rolaids are added to this concentrated stomach acid" followed by a plop and a fizz. Properly prepared, the listener will provide a video in her mind to fit the sound effect. That could easily be the only production needed for the entire spot.

The tendency for people to supply their own mental images to accompany identifiable sound effects has frequently been exploited commercially. One of the earliest and most successful uses of this technique was in the 1970s when the Dupont Corporation ran a series of television commercials for their Zerex brand antifreeze. The aim of the commercial was to demonstrate how Zerex contained a special ingredient that would automatically seal small holes in your radiator. The demonstration was graphic. The picture showed a close-up of a Zerex can. While the voice-over talked about how well the product protected radiators from accidental punctures, the picture showed a hand holding a sharp object. Three holes were punched in the can. Three streams of liquid, presumably Zerex, spurted from the holes. As this was happening, the sound track played three metallic crunches, each followed by the sound of liquid spraying. In an impressively short time, each of the liquid streams slowed and stopped. As each one slowed, the spraying sound diminished until, as the third stream dried up and stopped, so did the spraying sound. The message had been put across forcefully and believably. The commercial ran on television until Dupont's research showed a vast majority of people in the national television audience had seen the spot.

Then Dupont stopped buying television time, and instead bought time on national radio newscasts, time that costs much less than its television equivalent. The radio spot started off by blatantly announcing, "this is a radio commercial for a television commercial. No doubt, you've seen the Zerex commercial on TV in which we punch some holes in a can of Zerex. . ." As the voice on the radio said these words, the listeners heard the same metallic crunching followed by the spraying sound that had accompanied the television commercials. Every person who had seen the television commercial, when hearing the radio spot, mentally played back the video portion of the commercial in their imagination. Zerex, therefore, was able to buy what amounted to additional television time for the price of radio.

Sound effects are only effective if they are instantly identifiable by the listener. In the case of the Rolaids demonstration, we explain what is going to happen before it's heard. In the case of the Zerex spot, the listener was reminded of the television spot before the sounds from it were heard. Tony Schwartz tells of an experiment in which he found that, in a nursery school, the students were 75 percent more accurate than their teachers in distinguishing the sound of milk being poured into a glass from the sound of water being poured into the same type glass. The sound was an integral part of their everyday lives and totally familiar to them. Another example from Schwartz: Even to an experienced city-dweller, the sound of a garbage truck is, essentially, nothing more than a mechanical whir or whine. It could just as well be a bulldozer, an electric generator or a vacuum cleaner. As we've discussed, it would be possible to prepare the listener by referring to garbage trucks in the script immediately before the sound is heard. But another, and perhaps more effective way to distinguish the sound for the listener would be to include, at the beginning of the truck noise, the sound of a metal garbage can being banged against the side of the truck.

Sound effects can easily become intrusive and distracting, so be careful to use them as sparingly as possible. Your goal should be to hint, not to hit your listener over the head.

―――― LISTEN TO CUT 16 ON THE INSTRUCTIONAL TAPE.

Like sound effects, background music can help in creating a mood or feeling. Beware, though, as with sound effects, that you don't overdo the music. The tendency to use too much music in commercial production is exacerbated by exposure to locally written and produced spots on many radio stations where they practice what is sometimes referred to as "quick-and-dirty production." The client demands something more than simply handing the disc jockey a script to read, so the salesperson promises the spot will be "produced." Someone writes the spot and it is given to an announcer who takes it into a recording studio. She selects a record album from a bin of innocuous instrumentals. She throws the record on a turntable, and with the tape recorder running, plays the record and reads the spot. She fades out the music when she reaches the end of the copy and stops the tape machine. The spot has now been "produced" and the client is happy.

Such an approach to commercial production is sometimes necessary in the high-pressure, no-time-to-do-anything-right atmosphere of a local radio station. But for a voice-over demo tape—especially *your* demo tape—you should strive for a much higher standard of production quality. Each spot should, of course, be analyzed by asking the four basic questions. Your answer to the fourth question—what is the motivator—should lead you a long way toward determining what kind of mood you want to establish, what effect you want to have on your listener. Once you know this, you can start looking for music, or other production material, to help achieve your goal.

Where to Find Music

Film editor Ralph Rosenblum, who is responsible for editing such successful motion pictures as *Annie Hall* and *Goodbye Columbus,* as well as thousands of television commercials, tells in his book *When the Shooting Stops, the Cutting Begins* how, when he worked for the Office of War Information during the Second World War, he made the acquaintance of a man named Max Goberman. Goberman's job at the OWI was to find pre-recorded music to fit propaganda and military training films. According to Rosenblum, Goberman's entire stock of recordings consisted of five classical compositions. The first was Tchaikovsky's Sixth (Pathétique) Symphony. It has everything from themes of great pathos to a triumphal march full of great pride. Stravinsky's "Firebird Suite" has a troubling and frenzied sound as does Tchaikovsky's Fourth Symphony. Beauty and pain are both expressed in Rachmaninoff's Second Piano Concerto while Moussorgsky's "Pictures at an Exhibition" contains so many different moods, you really have to listen to it all the way through and then see what fits your needs. (Don't get the original piano version, get the orchestration by Maurice Ravel. Or, for a modern feeling, see if you can find the version of this work done on a Moog synthesizer or the recording by Emerson, Lake & Palmer.)

In addition to Goberman's original five selections, there are many compositions in the classical repertoire that can be effectively used as background music for commercials. To name but a few: If you need ethereal or angelic music, try Ravel's "Daphnis and Chlöe." For serious and stately music, nothing beats Elgar's "Pomp and Circumstance," unless it is Brahms' "Academic Festival Overture." Listen to some overtures from operas. Composers like Wagner, Offenbach, Puccini and Verdi wrote some powerful and stirring music. But operas aren't the only source of overtures. Listen to some of the overtures to Broadway shows. Stay away, though, from well-known shows like *Oklahoma, Sound of Music* or *Cats.* Older and less remembered shows still have very usable material in their overtures—shows like *They're Playing Our Song* or *How To Succeed In Business*

Without Really Trying. Even with the classics, you should avoid those that are so well known that they have become clichés. Remember the joke that defines an intellectual as someone who can listen to the "William Tell Overture" without thinking of the Lone Ranger. Likewise, anyone who has ever seen Walt Disney's *Fantasia* will find it most difficult to listen to "The Sorcerer's Apprentice" without picturing Mickey Mouse. And that, even though the listener conjures it up for himself, is vampire audio.

Sound track albums from motion pictures are also a good source of production music. Again, don't go for the big blockbuster movie. Everyone is totally familiar with the music from such films as *Dirty Dancing* and *Star Wars*.

Popular music can also be used, so long as it wasn't a best seller. Groups such as The Electric Light Orchestra can be used quite effectively. If you're looking for something with a down-home flavor, try the Charlie Daniels Band, the Earl Scruggs Review or Chet Atkins. Want nostalgia for a bygone era? Try some old big band or ragtime music (but avoid the more familiar Scott Joplin numbers. Since *The Sting* they've been played to death.) Ethnic music is frequently good for production. For example, an "oom-pah" band is great for a spot for German beer. An Irish jig is perfect for a spot about a Saint Patrick's Day sale.

Use your imagination. Just remember, don't use something that is so familiar it will distract attention from your voice-over work and, for the same reason, don't get too elaborate. Don't try, for example, to match phrases of dialogue with phrases of music. You want your listener to be impressed with how you sound, not how sexy your production is. Again, for the same reason, don't use vocals. It's your voice that's important, not the singer's. Moreover, words on top of words can be distracting and confusing. Your listener should always be paying attention to *you*, not the words of the song.

The first place to look for music is your own record collection and that of friends. Record stores are obvious sources, but pick a big store and check out the dusty bins in the back. You may be surprised by what treasures you'll find. Of course, it doesn't make sense to spend money buying records when they are available for free, so check your local public library. Many libraries have music departments where you can listen to various recordings. If you find something you think will work, and it is in good condition, borrow it. Library recordings, though, lead a rough life. So don't just listen to the music. Be alert to the possible presence of scratches, hiss, pops and other surface noise that can make the record unusable for your purposes. Even if the library record isn't usable, you've at least done your research and know what record to buy.

Once you have found the appropriate music and sound effects, make a second draft of your tape, and this time, include whatever production you feel might be appropriate, playing it in the background while you read the individual spots. As usual, get feedback on your efforts and revise your work accordingly.

11 – Making the Reel

Once you have your spots selected and have assembled your production material, it's time to head for the studio. Call a number of studios in your area and explain what you want to do. Ask for their prices. In New York, for example, a fairly typical recording studio currently charges one hundred dollars an hour for studio recording and slightly less for production. These prices include the services of an audio engineer but do not include the cost of blank tape and reels.* Some studios charge separately for the engineer. Should the studio have its own library of production music

---

* Although they charge extra for audio tape, most studios will not permit you to provide your own. There's a good reason: different brands and types of tape have different magnetic characteristics and, to get the most lifelike reproduction, a tape recorder should be adjusted to meet the characteristics of the tape you are using. A studio will generally use only one specific brand and type of tape. All their equipment is adjusted to provide optimum performance with that particular tape. The tape you bring could result in an overly muddy or tinny sounding recording. It is really in your best interest for them to provide the tape and charge you for it.

or sound effects, there will be an additional charge for each use from their library. Some studios charge different rates for weekdays, evenings and weekends. Most studios have a minimum amount of time you must book and pay for, usually either an hour or thirty minutes. Almost all recording studios publish a rate card listing their charges for various services. Ask for one from each studio you talk with. Then, at your leisure, you can sit down and estimate what your particular recording session should cost. If there's something on the rate card you don't understand, call them and ask about it. They are in business to sell a service and will do anything within reason to get your patronage. So don't be afraid to ask.

There's no way you can nail down in advance exactly what it will cost to make your demo reel because there's no way to predict precisely how long it's going to take. You may plan on taking three hours in the studio and find yourself finished after two and a half. Then, again, it may take four or five hours. But, for planning purposes, you can use the following guidelines which are based on past experience with students making their first demo tape.

The average person can record the voice-track for four spots in approximately one hour. You may get lucky and get an acceptable take of a particular spot on the second or third try. But on another spot, you may have to struggle through ten or twelve or more takes before you're satisfied. Still, the average of an hour for four spots generally holds true. It follows that any additional spots will probably take an additional fifteen minutes each to record.

Doing the production on four spots should take about an hour and forty minutes. Don't assume that because you don't intend to do any production on one of your spots, you can plan less time. This average time is based on experience showing that, even when one spot isn't produced, there is usually another spot that will take extra time to do correctly. So plan on an hour and forty minutes for producing four spots, and an additional twenty-five minutes for each additional spot.

You should plan on allowing another twenty minutes to review the final mixed and edited master, making any final minor changes and making some duplicate copies, or *dubs.* So, if you intend to make a demo reel containing four spots, figure your prices based on an hour in the studio and two hours production. Even if that doesn't turn out to be accurate, you will have had a basis to compare studios and their prices.

In a given market, your price estimates, based on the rate cards, should be different from studio to studio, but they should all be in the same ballpark. If one studio seems to come out charging an outrageous amount more than all the others, check your figures. You may have overlooked something. If your figures check out, call them. It is possible their rate card is based on the assumption you will need (or not need) something other than what you want. Explain carefully what you want and go over your figures with them. If, for example, the studio normally records rock bands, their rates may be based on the assumption that you will be needing facilities for mixing multiple channels on eight or sixteen tracks. If you explain that all you require is a full-track, mono recording made at a speed of $7^{1}/2$ ips (inches per second) they may quote you a much lower price. If they don't, go elsewhere. There is no reason for you to pay exorbitant prices for equipment and facilities you don't need.

If, however, the price of one studio is substantially lower than all the others, beware. Check them out with someone not connected with that or any other studio: an engineer for a local radio station, the owner of a local stereo and audio equipment store, even the Better Business Bureau. If the low-price studio appears to be legitimate, go over your figures with them and, if they agree that you have it calculated correctly, get a written quote from them for the entire job. Otherwise, you may find yourself being charged with a series of after-the-fact fees you didn't anticipate.

If you are lucky enough to have a friend who has access to a radio station or recording studio, you may not have to pay anything more than the cost of supplying your own blank tape and reels. Many voice-over performers have had their demo tapes made late on Saturday or Sunday night with the help of a friend who works as the weekend announcer at a local radio station. Don't be ashamed to ask for help. It won't cost your friend anything, and let's face it, when you start handing out demo tapes right and left, it can get to be an expensive proposition. There's nothing wrong with cutting corners where you can, so long as the quality of the product doesn't suffer.

The Voice Track

The first thing to do when you begin your recording session is to cut the voice tracks. Don't worry about what order the spots will eventually be in. Start with whichever one you feel most comfortable doing. Record the spot and listen to the playback. Make whatever changes you feel are appropriate in your copy markings and try another take. Listen to that one. Keep trying different approaches until you are satisfied with a particular take.

When you finish the first spot, continue with the next one following the same procedure.

Sometimes you may decide, after eight takes, for example, that the best one was really the fifth take. No problem. The engineer will have kept each take so whatever one you finally decide upon can be separated from the rest and used in your final version. Just to be safe, though, make sure you keep track of how many takes you make of each spot and which one you ultimately picked. Don't try to remember; write in on the copy. With all the things going on, you won't be able to remember. Write it. Frequently, the engineer will also keep track of the number of takes and the one you want. Don't depend on it, though. Engineers are human and have been known to make mistakes. You keep track of what's going on—in writing!

Suppose you finish the fifth take and, when listening to the playback, you realize it was absolutely perfect except for the next to last sentence. So you go back and try it again. But this time, although you did the last several lines superbly, the early part of the spot fell flat on its face. Do you have to go on with a seventh, eighth, or more takes until you get it right? Definitely not! Pick a point somewhere in the spot where both takes were good and ask the engineer to edit the last part of take six onto the first part of take five. Voila! A perfect rendition of the spot. Isn't modern technology astounding?

Elsewhere in this text we mentioned that each and every word of a piece of copy is sacrosanct. The client and his producer know what they want to say and it is up to you to say it the way they want it said. You have no prerogative to add, omit, or alter a single word. All very true. However, when you are making your own demo tape, you are both the client and the producer, in addition to being the talent. So for one shining moment in what we hope will be your long career, you have the freedom to do whatever you want with the copy! If a phrase is creating impossible problems for you, change it. If it suddenly occurs to you that the meaning would be much clearer if you added a word, add it. If some other words seem superfluous or redundant, drop them. Reword things to your heart's content. After all, it's your own tape and who's to know? No agent, when listening to your tape, will ever stop and say "Wait a minute! Those aren't the words they used in the original spot!" Not unless you do something totally outrageous like changing Dupont's slogan "better things for better living through chemistry" to something like "improved objects for improved existence by using polymers." Common sense should dictate what you'll be able to get away with. But within those bounds, you're not only allowed to, you have an obligation to yourself to do whatever is necessary to make your tape sound as good as it possibly can.

Of course, most of the changes you make to the copy will have been decided upon long before you enter the studio. That's what practice sessions are for. In fact, all the decisions you make—whether about the copy, your delivery, the production you intend to use—any decision about anything at all, should be made in advance whenever possible. That's not to say you can never change your mind when you hear your spot for the first time on the studio's quality equipment. Nothing about this business of making a demo tape is ever set in concrete. On the other hand, wasting costly studio time not only makes the project more expensive than necessary, it also marks your amateur status.

Doing the Production

Once you have a satisfactory take on each of your spots, you get time to catch your breath while the engineer pulls the good take of each spot out from the others. Then you add the production.

Many record stores carry sound-effect records. If you have an effect that is available on one of these records, just bring it into the control room and give it to the engineer. It will help if you already know which side and which cut on the record you want to use. You should have already listened to the record at home and decided what particular sound effect fitted the copy. Studio time is far too expensive to spend listening to cut after cut on the record to decide which you want to use. The same holds true for musical selections. Make your decisions at home. You can then hand the engineer the recording without wasting a moment of the time for which you are paying so dearly.

The closer you can keep to the original source of your production material, the better it will sound. If, for example, the music comes on a record, don't go to the trouble of putting it on tape. You won't accomplish anything by way of convenience since the engineer can handle records just as easily as tapes. Besides, if you have ever used a photocopy machine, you know that the first copy looks almost as good as the original. But if you try to make a copy of the copy and compare that with the original, you can discern a loss of quality. Another generation or two of copies and the quality really begins to drop off. The same thing happens with audio recording; each time you make a copy of a copy, you lose more quality.

The closest you can come to the original source, of course, is the original source. So if you intend to use the sound of coffee pouring into a cup, actually bring a cup and saucer into the studio. Then, when you are doing the production (not while you're trying to read the copy) simply pour some liquid into the cup. Note that we suggested you bring a *cup and saucer* into the studio. Remember Tony Schwartz's experiments in which children were able to distinguish between the sounds of pouring milk and water? Well, the same principle holds true here. It probably won't make too much difference whether you pour coffee or water, but there certainly is a discernable difference between the sounds of liquid being poured into a drinking glass and into a cup. Putting the cup on a saucer also makes a difference in the sound.

Many other sound effects can best be done "live" in the studio. If your copy talks about the passage of time, a metronome or a wind-up kitchen timer can be just the right touch. If it's a wine commercial, bring a bottle and a corkscrew into the studio. Just remember, as in the case of the coffee cups, pouring wine into a drinking glass doesn't sound anything like the sound you get when you pour it into a wine glass. And use real crystal glasses, not those cheap plastic ones. They sound wrong for pouring and you can't clink them.

Even some musical production can be done "live." If your spot is for a baby care product, an inexpensive wind-up music box can prove to be a powerful mood enhancer. Just bring one with you to the recording session.

If the music is on a pre-recorded cassette, have the tape cued to the proper point so you and the engineer don't have to hunt for the right spot. Simply put the tape in your machine at home and play it until you reach the beginning of the music or sound effect you want to use. Right before it starts, stop the tape and, without rewinding, take it out of the tape machine and put it into its little plastic box. When you go into the studio, hand it to the engineer and tell him it is already cued. He'll appreciate the help, you'll look more professional and you'll both save a lot of time. It's important for you to have the cassette already cued because it's astonishing how much studio time can be used up by an engineer pushing buttons while you say things like "try it right there . . . no, that's not it . . . a little bit farther in . . . no . . . I think it's about two more cuts in . . . no, that's not it either . . . maybe we went too far. Go back a little . . . no, a little more . . . no . . . maybe it's after this part here . . ." Don't think it will happen to you? You're welcome to try it; you're paying for the studio time. But if you come into the studio with an uncued tape, you can bet your widowed grandmother's next pension check you'll be mimicking the monologue above.

Your cassette recorder has a booby trap built into it in the form of the little three-digit counter that keeps changing while the tape is moving. Some people think they count seconds. Some people assume they count the number of feet the tape has traveled. Well, surprise! They don't count anything at all; they're completely arbitrary. They were put there solely as a way for you to rewind the tape to a certain point so you can play it again. The booby trap, though, is in the fact that those little numbers are *so* arbitrary that the counter on your machine has only the most casual and coincidental relationship, if any at all, to the counter on any other machine. Consequently, although you can come pretty close to the point in the tape you need by fast-forwarding the tape to, say, 125 on your counter, you'll find that it only works on your machine. Give a tape to the studio engineer with instructions to cue it up to 125 on the counter and you will be unpleasantly surprised to find a piece of music you have no use for whatsoever. Then you'll be back to the old "that's not it, go back a little . . . no, a little more . . . no . . . try fast forward . . ."

Music on pre-recorded cassettes is, for all practical purposes, as acceptable as a record or compact disc. The quality of all three is more than sufficient to provide professional sounding results. But, beware of using your own homemade cassettes. If your cassette machine is a high-quality console model that is either an integral part of your stereo system or a component electronically interconnected with your stereo, you may be able to get an off-the-air recording that's good enough to use for production purposes. Don't expect, however, to get any kind of usable quality by taking your portable machine and putting the mike in front of the speaker of your radio. It won't work, because there will be too much loss of quality and you'll be introducing room noise into the recording.

For the same reason, don't try to record your own sound effects. If you need the sound of a kitchen appliance, bring it with you to the studio. If you need the sound of downtown traffic, boats on the river, or children laughing, get them from a sound-effects recording.

There are two reasons for all this emphasis on the technical quality of your production material. The first reason is we want to preserve that willing suspension of disbelief—the tacit agreement between you and the listener to pretend these are spots you actually did for professional use. If the tape doesn't sound good enough technically to have been of professional quality, you run the risk of shattering the illusion. After all, that's why you're using a professional studio in the first place. If technical excellence didn't matter, you could have just as well stayed at home and made your tape on your little portable cassette machine.

The second reason for emphasizing technical quality is the nature of the equipment on which the tape will be played. Some of the larger agencies and casting departments have superb equipment. They will be able to hear the slightest flaw, the smallest pop or click, the quietest hiss or hum. The people who use this equipment have become used to quality sound, and it is to your advantage to give it to them. There's no sense in letting them be distracted by technical problems, another kind of vampire audio.

On the other end of the quality spectrum are those agents who opened their offices thirty or thirty-five years ago and have, since then, seen no need to update any of their equipment. "If it still works, why throw it out?" seems to be their credo. The sound quality of their old tape machines leaves much to be desired. Moreover, it leaves much of your superb performance on the tape, unheard. There isn't much you can do about their equipment, but you can minimize the damage done to your tape by starting with the highest quality sound possible. Even after being degraded by poor equipment, it will still sound pretty decent. But if the technical quality is minimal to start with, by the time it gets through some of the antiquated tape machines on which it will have to be heard, it can do you more harm than good.

Every audio engineer has his own way of working, and it won't accomplish much for you to tell him how to go about mixing your tape. But he's there to come up with a product that will be pleasing to you, so you should explain at the very beginning what results you want. If, on playback, you feel what you've heard isn't quite what you want, explain why it isn't right yet and he'll do it again. And again, until you are satisfied with the results. Remember, don't tell him *how* to go about his job, but don't be the least bit hesitant about explaining what results you want, and keep insisting upon them until you get them.

Some engineers will sit there and do whatever you say. Their attitude is that they are a hired hand and you are the boss, and whatever you want to do is fine with them. But some engineers occasionally offer suggestions. If the engineer is mature and appears to have been in the business a long time, it may be to your advantage to give those suggestions careful consideration.

An important thing to listen for in production is the balance between voice and production, especially music. The best reading in the world can be ruined if it is partially drowned-out by the music. If there is the slightest doubt about the music volume, ask that the spot be redone with the music level just a little lower. If you're still unsure, take the music level another notch lower and try again.

In addition to the large, expensive, super-fidelity speakers normally used during a recording session, many studios are equipped to also let you listen on a small, cheap, speaker that simulates a portable or car radio. Ask if they have one of these little speakers and, if they do, ask for a playback through that as a final check.

Mixing the production material with your voice track can be an exhilarating or frustrating experience, depending on how well you have prepared. If your choices of music and sound effects work anywhere near as well as you had hoped you'll, literally, want to jump for joy. If, however, you miscalculated and the production you've chosen doesn't seem to work with the copy for some reason, you'll become upset, frustrated, and even depressed. If it happens to you, don't panic. Remember it's always better to have no production at all than to have poor production. So leave the voice track alone. You can always come back later with new production material and mix the spot again. It may cost you a few extra dollars, but it will be well worth it to have a good tape.

Whatever you do, don't settle for second best in the voicing and production of your demo tape. It is vitally important that you be completely and totally satisfied with every bit of it. If there is anything at all you are less than delighted with, you will subconsciously use that as an excuse not to put forth your best effort in marketing yourself. So make sure your demo tape is something you can be proud to have anyone listen to. If you aren't completely satisfied with a voice track, keep doing it until you are. If the production isn't precisely what you want, mix it again until you are satisfied.

Once you are completely delighted with each individual cut, and convinced that nobody in the world could possibly do these spots better than you have, you're ready to assemble them into a demo reel. Decide which is your best cut. Lead off with that one. Each subsequent spot should contrast with the one that precedes it. Listen to the final result. Pay attention to how one spot flows into another, how the production as well as your delivery provides variety and contrast from one spot to another. If it doesn't work to your satisfaction, try another arrangement. Keep trying until you're positive the order is right.

—— LISTEN TO CUT **17** ON THE INSTRUCTIONAL TAPE.

Mixing the Reel

The voice master is made first. Once you have your voice master finished, and the perfect takes edited out, you mix in the production, and the result is the final-mix master tape or, simply, the master. By definition, a master is an original from which copies are made, but even a master can, in reality, be a copy. The voice master may be a true original recording, but, by adding the production, you have created a sub-master which, in the case of the voice, is now *second generation.* If your music came from an LP record, it is already at least a half-dozen or so generations away from the original. It is impossible to escape the need to make copies of copies, but if the equipment used is of the best quality and great care is employed in using that equipment, the amount of quality loss can be kept to a minimum, so it may be many generations before the degradation becomes noticeable.

All professional recording (except some forms of digital, which don't concern us) is done on what are called *reel-to-reel* machines. The name is pretty descriptive; you put a reel of blank tape on the left side of the recorder and thread the end of the tape through the recording heads and onto an empty take-up reel on the right side. As the recording progresses, the tape is transported from the left side (the *feed reel*) through the head assembly, which is the part that does the actual recording, and onto the take-up reel. The speed at which tape moves across the recording heads has a lot to do with the quality of the recording. It's axiomatic that, all other things being equal, the higher the tape speed, the less loss of quality between original and recording.

For many years, the tape speed for professional recording has been standardized at two speeds: 7$\frac{1}{2}$ ips and 15 ips. The lower speed (7$\frac{1}{2}$ ips) gives reasonably good quality, and therefore is adequate for many purposes. It has two other advantages: it's economical because you use only half as much tape, and 7$\frac{1}{2}$

ips is compatible with less expensive home model reel-to-reel machines which operate at 7$\frac{1}{2}$ and 3$\frac{3}{4}$ ips. The higher speed on professional machines, 15 ips, gives maximum quality and is always used when making masters. It is also used for making submasters. In fact, until you get around to making your final dubs, *everything* should be done at 15 ips.

When you are completely satisfied with the final mixed master, it's time to make the dubs. Since most agents don't have large, expensive, professional tape recorders at their disposal, your tape will most likely be listened to on a home-variety tape machine. As already pointed out, these machines can accommodate a top tape speed of only 7$\frac{1}{2}$ ips. Your dubs, therefore, should all be made at that speed.

You will want to make a few cassette copies as well. Tape speed is no problem here since all cassettes run at the same speed. Almost all agents and casting departments want reel-to-reel tapes but, in recent years, a growing minority of them are converting to cassettes. You will want to have enough cassettes so when you're asked for one, you can produce it immediately. There are other reasons you'll want a few cassette copies of your demo tape that we'll deal with later. But certainly, one reason is you'll need to show your mother what you've been working on these last few months, so hard that you've been too busy to call her.

Dubs should be put on five-inch reels and stored in matching boxes. The recording studio can provide these for you. The master, so it doesn't get confused with a dub, should be put on a seven-inch reel. Actually, you should keep two masters; the final mix-down and the original voice master. If you want more dubs, take the mixed master to any recording studio (or radio station where you have a friend) and have them cranked out. The voice-track master, also on a seven-inch reel, is insurance in case anything should ever happen to the final master. Should it be necessary, you could go back and remix your master without having to re-cut the voice track; you'd only have to replicate the production. Yet another reason for keeping the voice-track master:

If, months later, you should discover a piece of music that is far superior to the production you originally used on one of your spots, you can take the new production and the voice-track master to a studio and have a new mix done. This new mix can then be edited into your final master to replace the original spot at far less than the cost of a complete recording session.

One final note: Should the recording studio offer to keep the master in their files for you, pleasantly and politely decline their kind offer. If they tell you everyone does it that way, be adamant. Insist on taking it with you. After all, it's your tape. You paid for it, you own it, and you have a right to do anything you want with it—including taking it to another studio to have more dubs made because you can get the job done less expensively.

Once you get the dubs home, you have to label them—inside and out. Outside labeling should include, at the very least, your name and phone number. This basic information should be put on the front and all four edges of the box. Thus, no matter how the tape is stored on a shelf, your name and number is still visible. Everyone agrees on the necessity of this basic information. Beyond that, however, it's a matter of opinion as to what information should be included on the box. Here are the arguments pro and con; you'll have to decide what's best in your particular situation.

Some people put their picture on the front of the box. The rationale is that the picture reminds the agent or casting director who you are so that you aren't just another voice in the crowd. The desired reaction is something along the lines of "Oh, yeah. That's the blond with horn-rimmed glasses" or "That's right. He's the bald guy with the beard." The idea is to personalize you even before they get to the business of listening. The main objection is that printing labels with pictures is expensive, and besides, it doesn't matter what you look like. The only important thing is how you sound. If the listener has too concrete an image of what you look like, she might not be able to imagine you doing a spot that you sound great for, but you don't necessarily look right for.

The other item about which there is some disagreement concerning tape labels is listing the contents. Some people ignore the subject entirely while others feel it necessary to indicate what the tape contains. One school of thought is that casting people, when casting a voice-over for a given product—soft drinks, perhaps—will look for people who have done spots for soft drinks before. This gives rise to the question of whether you give specific brand names or just generic product categories. Generic advocates hypothesize that if a casting director looking for a spokesperson for Coca-Cola sees Pepsi on your label of contents, he won't even listen to your demo tape. So there are three common formats for tape labels. Two of them are:

PEPSI COLA		SOFT DRINK
CHEVROLET		AUTOMOBILE
MACYS	or	DEPARTMENT STORE
SONY TV		TELEVISION SET

The third school of thought rejects both arguments. The theory here is that the demo tape is a general demonstration of your ability. If they want to know if you have product exclusivity in a particular category, they will ask you or your agent about it before they call you in for an audition. There is no sense in categorizing yourself before the fact.

Labels can be simple self-adhesive, or "press-apply," on which you have typed the necessary information. This, however, is the minimum you can get away with. Don't try to use hand lettering on your boxes. No matter how steady your hand, it still looks tacky and unprofessional. Some people get a rubber stamp made and use it on all their tapes. It can produce good results if you are careful to let it dry before you touch it. Otherwise, it may smudge, which will look worse than hand-lettered labels. A more elaborate kind of label follows (reduced in size). When cut out with an Exacto knife and attached to the top of the box with rubber cement, it makes for a very professional presentation. When the original artwork or layout has been done, labels can be

ADRIAN CRONAUER JU2-4240

ADRIAN CRONAUER JU2-4240

VOICE-OVERS

ADRIAN CRONAUER

JU2-4240

ADRIAN CRONAUER JU2-4240

ADRIAN CRONAUER   JU2-4240

printed in quantity at relatively low cost. You may also want to consider printing your labels in color to make them stand out even more.

The reels should also be labeled. It's too easy for the tape to get separated from the box. The easiest way to label the reel is to get $1/2'' \times 1^{3/4}''$ self-adhesive labels from your local stationery store. They come in boxes of 840 sheets with twenty-one labels per sheet. Simply type your name and phone number on each label and stick one on each reel.

Make Your Tape

After reading to this point and doing all the exercises suggested, you should be ready to actually make a demo reel. Go ahead and book a studio. Make the tape, ordering as many copies as you expect to hand out in the first month or two. Make up the labels, affix them to the reels and boxes, and get ready to start marketing yourself as outlined in the next chapter.

A word of advice: Do not overpractice before going to the studio. Too much practice can lock you into a single interpretation and prevent you from profiting from last-minute inspiration and insight or from suggestions from the engineer.

Remember, there is nothing to be worried about. You have been well trained, you are better prepared than a vast majority of people who make demo tapes and you should produce a fine tape. If nervousness does become a problem, remember your deep breathing exercises. Of course, you most certainly *do not* want to use a cocktail or a tranquilizer to calm yourself down. Any kind of chemical depressant will only take the edge off your concentration, and will mean the difference between what could be a truly great tape and one that is only acceptable.

Get a good night's sleep the night before and eat lightly the day of the recording session.

GOOD LUCK!

Marketing Yourself

Nobody wants to fail, but some people try harder than others.

. . . Robert Half

I—Factors for Success

Conventional wisdom holds that the way to succeed in any performing art is to have talent, training, and ability. Well, as in so many areas, the conventional wisdom is only partially correct. There are hundreds, if not thousands, of people with great talent, gobs of ability, and superb training who are working as cab drivers and waitresses because they don't have the determination and tenacity necessary to pursue a career in voice-overs (or, for that matter, in any other performing art). Just because you are talented, just because you have ability, don't think you can sit back and wait for the offers to pour in. It doesn't work that way. There are more talented people than there are available jobs. In addition to all those perfectly qualified people, there are scores of people who have limited, if any ability at all. Their ambition far exceeds their competence. They are competing with you for the attention of agents and casting directors. These driven but untal-

ented people make it even harder for you, the truly able performer, to get through the defenses the casting people have built
around themselves as a matter of pure survival.

You, as a potential voice-over performer, have to break
down the defenses of the casting people and present yourself as a
desirable commodity. But, before you can break down their defenses, you have to break down your own. We all have inhibitions.
We all have defense mechanisms. One of the strongest of our defense mechanisms is avoidance. When presented with the possibility of an unpleasant situation, we tend to avoid it. Now, having
doors slammed in your face—either metaphorically or literally—
is not a pleasant experience. Yet much of the business of voice-
overs, at least at first, consists of dealing with just this kind of
rejection. Lots and lots of rejection! Once we realize what we are
up against, it becomes very easy to find reasons why we shouldn't
go see that particular agent, why we don't need to make that
phone call just yet.

When tempted to postpone unpleasant tasks, there are a
number of tried-and-true maxims and stories you should remember. One is that a decision not to make a decision is, in itself, a
decision. Think about it: A decision not to make a decision is, in
itself, a decision.

A great aphorism states: "Delay is the deadliest form of
denial." When a student protested that he didn't understand
what that meant, the professor countered, "I'll be glad to explain
it to you, but our classtime has run out. Ask me again tomorrow."

In his autobiography, Benjamin Franklin tells of how he
and some friends were out on the water in a boat. One of the people on the boat had become quite drunk and refused to row. The
others insisted that he share in the rowing chores, but the drunk-
ard refused, pointing out that if the others wished to reach shore,
someone would have to row, and whether he, individually, partici-
pated in the effort or not, they would all reach shore together. After much discussion, Franklin—ever the pragmatist—tipped the
wastrel overboard and suggested that if he did not choose to row,
perhaps he could swim to shore. The story has an application in

the situation of the person marketing himself. It is easy enough and quite valid for each person in a rowboat to reason that he, individually, doesn't need to row. Yet, if nobody rows, the boat will stay dead in the water. Similarly, it is easy to tell yourself that no real harm will be done if you put off making that phone call, or going to see that particular agent, today. So far, you are quite correct. You can always do it tomorrow. The trouble comes when the tomorrows start to pile up and you haven't made the call. The more you put it off, the easier it is to continue to procrastinate.

Just as Alcoholics Anonymous insists on the ironclad rule that a reformed drinker is never to take even that first drink, so those who are inclined to procrastinate must decide for themselves that it will be an inviolable rule never to postpone a call or visit to an agent or casting director.

One of the most useful mindsets you can adopt is to realize that you are engaged in a business. Like any other business, you have to keep regular hours and, during those hours, pursue the business you are in with single-minded determination. Set up routines and schedules for yourself and stick to them. We'll have more specific hints for you later in this chapter, but for the moment, remember that in business, the success you can expect is in direct proportion to the time and effort you put forth.

So keep in mind that the single most important factor in determining your success as a voice-over performer is your own motivation. Only you can provide the drive, determination and tenacity necessary to be successful.

There is an adage in the advertising profession that no advertising campaign, no matter how powerful, can make a consumer buy a product a second time. Consumers might be willing to give a new product a try, but if it doesn't live up to its claims, they will reject it out of hand. The same principle applies to marketing yourself. With enough persistence, you can probably manage to get through to any agent and convince him to send you out for an audition or two. If, however, you don't perform well, you will be dropped like the proverbial hot potato.

As important as motivation is in pursuing a career in

voice-overs, it isn't enough by itself. You have to have the ability to back it up. That ability has three facets: talent, training, and practice.

Natural talent is what you are born with. Much like your height, or the color of your hair and eyes, you're stuck with what the Good Lord gave you. To use an analogy from the world of music, some people have perfect pitch while others couldn't carry a tune in a bucket. Similarly, some people seem to have a natural flair for verbal communication. Others have a stilted or monotonous way of talking, even when they are engaged in extemporaneous conversation. Think of how former Secretary of State Henry Kissinger sounds; there is little that could be done to make him over into a successful voice-over performer. The raw material simply isn't there.

Assuming, however, that the basic raw materials are there, they still have to be refined. The material in this book is designed to help you do just that. You have been exposed to the fundamental principles and techniques of copy interpretation. But that's only a foundation upon which you can build. The more training you have, the better you will be at your craft. Take classes if they are available or get private coaching if you can afford it. Work on your voice and diction—particularly diction. Don't stop there, though. Any kind of acting training will be of help, because voice-over is just a form of acting. Voice-over performers exercise the same skills as an actor; they take someone else's words from paper and try to convey those words to a listener both naturally and believably. The only thing to beware of is that conventional acting training places a lot of emphasis on projection. As we've discussed thoroughly, with voice-overs there is no need to project. On the contrary, your goal should be to under-project, since your listener's ear is as close as the microphone.

As with any skill, you'll get rusty unless you constantly practice. Make it a habit to regularly work on your voice-overs. Get new copy and analyze it, mark it, record it, listen to it, record it again, listen, and record again. Review, from time to time, the previous chapters in this book. Don't ever assume you have reached a point of perfection where you haven't any further need of practice and refinement. There's an old saying about how it's impossible to stand still. If you aren't going forward, you have to be slipping back. That old saying couldn't be truer than in the field of voice-overs. You must keep honing your skills.

So now we have isolated two distinct factors that are important in achieving success in voice-overs; motivation, and talent or ability. But that's not all. There is yet another factor to consider: plain old dumb luck—being in the right place at the right time. It does happen that a person gets a job simply because the agent or director needed someone quickly, didn't have the time to audition a lot of people, and grabbed the nearest person who seemed to be reasonably qualified.

In summary, then, these are the three factors vital to your success in voice-overs (in descending order of importance): motivation, talent, and luck. You can have all three and still not make it to the top, but leave out any one of the three and you most certainly will not be successful. The first two are up to you. The third is something you have no control over, except that you must be prepared to take advantage of any good luck that comes your way.

11 – Getting Your Start

Agents

One of the most common questions asked by people trying to break into the voice-over field is "do I need an agent?" The answer, like the answer to many questions about this field, is an unqualified "yes and no." Most people who are just getting their start will begin by calling on small agencies and production houses. With these smaller organizations, it is quite possible to get work without ever having to go through an agent. You simply give them your tape, call them regularly, follow our other suggestions on how to market yourself and, eventually, they'll call you for a job.

With the larger agencies and production houses, it's a different story. These organizations have found it far more efficient to deal exclusively through agents. Instead of listening to hundreds of demo tapes to find the types they want and then making dozens of phone calls to get people to audition, casting directors for the larger agencies simply make four or five calls to agents who they know handle top-rate talent. Each agent sends ten or twelve people and from those people, the choice is made.

If you ever intend to get into the voice-over big leagues, you will have to deal with agents.

What Do They Do?

An agent, above and beyond all else, gets you work. Not always; but without them, it would be a lot harder to get work, and you'd get it a lot less often. Theoretically, the agent works for you and in your best interest. In addition to sending you out on auditions, the agent is the one who negotiates the terms under which you will work, including, most importantly, how and what you are to be paid. Since the agent is compensated according to what you are paid, it is in her best interest to wrangle the best deal possible for you.

In addition to the formal requirements of the performer-agent relationship, a good agent will be able to give you advice and counseling about your career and the specifics of your vocal technique. One of the greatest things about an agent is she will tell you the truth. The next best thing about an agent is she will lie to you. One of the worst things about an agent is she will lie to you. The next worst thing is she will tell you the truth.

Even though the agent is, supposedly, working for you, she also values her relationship with the casting people, and if they don't seem too receptive to the idea of using you, the agent always has other talent she can suggest. She can hardly be expected to put her relationship with the casting directors in jeopardy for the sake of a single, new, untested performer. So don't expect too much from an agent. Always remember that the primary responsibility for marketing yourself lies on your own shoulders.

Since an agent works for you, you are the one who pays her. Anytime the agent gets work for you, she is entitled to ten percent of whatever payment she negotiates for you. "What?" says an occasional beginner, "You mean I have to give ten percent of everything I make to an agent?" Yes, you do! And the system works quite nicely, on the whole. You are going to get a vast majority of your work through agents, and, as the old maxim states, ninety percent of something is far preferable to a hundred percent of nothing.

An economist would look at it this way: a voice-over for a commercial has a specific worth—a dollar value. As an intermediary, the agent is entitled to something; after all, she has to make a living, too. If she weren't paid by you, the advertising agencies would have to pay her, and since the value of your work as a voice-over is only worth so many dollars, if the agency were to pay your agent, they would have to reduce the amount they pay to you. Think of the commercial budget as a pie. There is only so much money in the budget to produce a specific commercial. Since it is impossible to increase the overall size of the pie, it follows that the size of the piece allotted to voice-over costs is also fixed. When you get your slice of the pie, you are expected to cut off a tenth of it and give it to your agent. Were the system arranged so that the advertising agency, rather than you, paid your agent, the pie still wouldn't get any bigger. The agency would simply have to cut off the tenth of your slice before you got it, and you'd still wind up with the same amount of pie. With the agent working for you instead of the advertising agency, you are arguably better off, because the agent's interests and yours are interconnected.

Actually, there is one circumstance where the agent

doesn't really get paid by you. If the best the agent can negotiate for you is to do the job for scale (the minimum amount allowed under union contract) your agent is paid by the advertising agency. That way, you never wind up with the net amount in your pocket amounting to less than union scale.

Getting an Agent

Getting an agent to send you out on auditions is both simple and difficult. It's simple because all you have to do is go around to see agents and get them to listen to your tape. Agents, after all, need people to send out, so they are always looking for new talent they can peddle. If they think that you, on the basis of your tape, have the potential to make money for them and yourself, they will be only too happy to send you out under their auspices. The difficulty comes in getting the agents to listen to you, and convincing them that you are, indeed, a marketable commodity. It takes salesmanship, tenacity and persistence. Lots and lots of persistence.

Finding an agent is as simple as picking up the yellow pages. Finding a good agent is a little more difficult. You're getting involved in a relationship that will affect your career. Despite the fact that it is, assuredly, a business relationship, there has to be a certain amount of personal interaction. If the chemistry isn't right between you—if the karma is wrong—you'll be aware of it from the first meeting. She may be the most successful agent in the business, but if you don't get along well, there's no sense in pursuing the matter any further.

There are many legitimate and trustworthy agents. Sad to say, however, there are also a number of less than reputable people who claim to be agents, but in reality, are charlatans who prey on the inexperience of young hopefuls. To protect yourself, check out the agents you are considering before you commit yourself to any sort of business relationship. Call the local Better

Business Bureau and see if they have had any complaints about the agent in question. You don't have to be a member to ask AFTRA and SAG what they know about a particular agent. They may not be able to guarantee that he's reputable, but if he is a notoriously bad egg, they will know about it.

There is one ironclad rule you can depend upon when dealing with agents: *an agent NEVER makes money until YOU make money.* If an agent tells you he will need advance payment as a registration fee, an enrollment fee, payments to a recording studio or a photographer, or for whatever other reason, you can be sure the man is a fraud! Run—don't walk—to the nearest exit! Legitimate agents are *never* paid anything by you until they get you work, and then they only get ten percent of what you are paid. Never pay a single red cent to an agent until that agent has gotten you a job.

Signing Vs. Free-Lancing

If you are very good at what you do, and if you develop a rapport with a particular agent, you might be invited to sign a contract with that agent by which you agree to be represented by that agent exclusively. Should you do it? Opinions vary. The primary advantage to signing with one agent is that if the agent has a proprietary interest in you, he will be far more motivated to further your career. When an advertising agency calls an agent for talent to audition, the agent will usually send out people from his list of signed performers. Only after those on his list have all been contacted, will he begin to call others; the free-lancers.

Those who advise against signing with a single agent point out that no agent is capable of maintaining good relationships with all the possible sources of work. Veteran voice-over performer Jackson Beck—whose voice is known throughout the United States for his commercials for such products as Sominex, Meineke Mufflers and Hasbro Toy's G.I. Joe doll—has been doing voice-overs since the 1940s and has never signed with an agent. Speaking at a seminar held by the New York local of AF-TRA, Beck explained why: "I free-lance; I'm not signed. I wouldn't advise anybody in the voice-over business to sign with one agent, because no one agent has all the entree that you need. One agent may do business with a dozen advertising agencies, but there are a hundred advertising agencies out there that that agent can't get into anymore than you can." Many other prominent voice-over performers are, like Beck, free-lancers, presumably for the same reason.

To some extent, geography will dictate your decision whether to sign or to free-lance. In smaller markets, there are few, if any, agents so the question never arises—everybody free-lances. In Los Angeles, nobody free-lances; if you work at all, you must be signed to a specific agent. In New York, you have a choice; you can sign or free-lance as you wish. One producer-director put it this way: "In California, it's like a monogamous marriage. In New York, it's somewhere between an open relationship and free love."

Casting Directors

At any of the larger advertising agencies you will find a group of people who compose what is called the casting department. Individually, they are called casting directors. When a producer has a commercial developed to the point that she is ready to pick people to play the on-camera roles and to do the off-camera voice-overs, she calls the casting department, or sends them a written request, specifying what types are required. It is then the responsibility of the casting department to provide the producer with a choice of several people who might fit the specifications. Auditions, on video tape for the on-camera performers and audio tape for the voice-overs, are given to the producer. She selects one or more of the auditions, which are sent to the client for final approval. Once the talent has been approved by the client, the casting director calls each approved person's agent and gives them the happy news that their performer has a job.

Sometimes the choice is narrowed down to a few performers, but the producer and/or the client can't make a decision. You are asked to come back for another audition. For the performer, the call-back is a frustrating experience, since you will be doing, essentially, the same thing you did at the original audition. It can be viewed as encouraging, since it obviously means they liked you enough on the first audition to ask you to come back for the semifinals. You will also have to deal with what is known as the request for first refusal. What this means is, if you accept the first refusal, you agree not to book any other job on the same date that the agency has scheduled for doing the spot for which you have auditioned. Should you get another offer for work for that same time, you must give the original producer the courtesy of telling her what has happened. She, then, has the option of saying "yes, we want you" which becomes a firm booking or "no, we do not choose to exercise our right of first refusal" in which case, you are free to take the other booking.

Many of the smaller advertising agencies don't have enough production going on from day to day to justify paying a full-time salary to one or more casting directors. Instead of maintaining a full-time casting department, they engage the services of an independent casting agency. Such an organization functions the same way as the larger agency's casting department in that they consult with a commercial producer as to what qualities are required of talent for a proposed commercial, and then try to find performers who meet the criteria specified by the producer. From the standpoint of the performer, there is little difference between an agency's casting department and an independent casting agency. The process is the same and the end result is the same: if the producer and the client think you are right for the job, you get it. If they don't, you don't. The advertising agency pays the casting service, not you. So it doesn't make any real difference to you if you are auditioned by the agency's own casting department or an independent casting service.

Take My Tape...Please!

Getting agents and casting directors to listen to your tape isn't easy, but it is essential. You accomplish it by a process known as *making rounds*—a term used to describe calling on the offices of agents and casting directors. Your purpose is to get them to listen to your tape. If you can't get them to listen to it immediately, leave the tape and get a promise that they will listen to it at their earliest opportunity. Then follow up with phone calls until they have actually heard it. Most agents get tapes all the time. They let them pile up until they have several dozen. Then they spend an entire morning or afternoon listening to them. If your tape gets to them just after they have done one of these listening sessions, it may be another month or two before they get around to listening again. What is needed from you is patience and persistence.

Some performers carry a small cassette machine with them when they make rounds. In the machine is their demo tape on cassette. If they are lucky enough to get through to the agent herself, they whip out the little cassette machine and push the "play" button. It eliminates making a lot of phone calls only to hear, "I haven't had a chance to listen to your tape yet."

Publications

There are a number of publications you should be familiar with. Pick up and read through *Broadcasting, Billboard, Back Stage,* and *Variety.* Los Angeles talent will want to regularly read *Hollywood Reporter.* If you intend to work in New York City, you will need a copy of *Ross Reports: Television.* It is a monthly listing of all agents and casting directors in New York along with their addresses, phone numbers, and a description of what kind of talent they handle. Many of the listings include prohibitions such as "don't phone." Quite frankly, if you are timid enough to let such a warning prevent you from calling an agent, you should probably consider a different line of work.

A big help in making rounds is a book called the *Geographical Casting Guide*. It lists agents and casting directors by street address. By using this book, you can plan your activities efficiently. You can call on all the people who have offices in a given vicinity instead of spending all your time on buses and subways.

Both *Ross Reports* and the *Geographical Casting Guide* are specific to New York. In other markets, you may have to do your own research and make up your own lists or maps, but the effort is well worth it. Like any other business, you will achieve maximum results if you organize your work and structure your daily activities.

Another lesson you should learn from the world of business is the value of keeping adequate and accurate records. There is nothing more embarrassing than to call an agent for an appointment only to have him tell you that you have already scheduled an appointment next week. It is unrealistic to expect to be able to keep track of all the agents you talk with and to remember what was said. The only way to keep track of it all is to set up a record-keeping system. You can use something as simple as a card file or as complicated as a computer database program. The important thing is that your records be systematic, accurate and complete. For each agent and casting director you have had any contact with whatsoever, make a separate file card or page in some sort of ledger book or a computer entry. Include the agency name, the person contacted, their address, phone number, and any other pertinent information. Then, each and every time you have an occasion to contact that person whether by mail, phone or in person, note it in their file. Indicate when the contact was made, what was said, and what you should do, and when, as a follow-up. Also make a note on your calendar for the date when you should make the next follow-up call or visit. When that date comes, you have only to look at the file to refresh your memory. Of course, no matter how elaborate a record-keeping system you have, it won't be worth a thing if it doesn't contain complete and accurate information. So, make it a regular part of each day's business activity to update your file of agents and casting directors.

Postcards and Other Gimmicks

Why do national advertisers spend millions of dollars a year to do nothing more than keep the name of their product in the public eye? Why do Virginia Slims cigarettes underwrite tennis tournaments? Why did Dewars' Scotch sponsor a series of concerts at Carnegie Hall? Why does the manufacturer of Kool cigarettes pay for a substantial part of a yearly jazz festival? Why do Mobil Oil, TRW and other corporate giants pay for programming on public television when all they get is a mention at the beginning and end of the program? Because they all realize the value of *name recognition*. Similarly, you have a great interest in having your name become familiar in the microcosm of agents and casting directors. Anything you can do to promote your own name recognition will only be to your advantage; the more imaginative you are in your efforts, the better.

The most inexpensive way to keep your name prominent is by mailing out postcards. Some performers put their picture on one side of the postcard, but it isn't really necessary. The important thing is that you send them. Each time you talk with an agent, even on the phone, follow up with a card. Any holiday is an excuse for a card: Christmas, Easter, Fourth of July, Saint Swithens' Day...whatever the occasion, fire off another card. Should you get an audition, it is obligatory to send the agent a card saying "thanks" for getting you the audition and another to the casting director saying "thanks" for the opportunity to read for him. If you actually get a job, the same applies, but, in addition, you will send everyone on your list a card telling them about your booking and asking them to be looking for the spot to be on the air soon.

Any innovation you can come up with will increase your name recognition. Among the gimmicks used by some voice-over performers are inexpensive pens or pencils embossed with the performer's name and phone number, key chains with the same information, and one of the most inexpensive and effective ideas, your name and phone number printed on business cards that have been die-cut so they can be inserted right into a Rolodex. Even better, printed on colored cards so they stand out when they are put into the Rolodex.

Getting the Message

If you are doing your job properly, you can't afford to sit at home all day waiting for the phone to ring. You have to get out and make rounds. So what happens when an agent calls you for an audition? You must have some way of getting the agent's message. Your spouse, roommate or aged mother might be a possible solution. But, in most cases, you're going to wind up with a choice of either an answering machine or an answering service.

In the past few years, advances in electronic technology have remade answering machines from what was little better than a tape recorder attached to your phone line into an astounding marvel of computer design. Today, a relatively inexpensive answering machine can play an outgoing message of any length you choose, record an incoming message of any length you choose or until the caller has finished talking. You can call home from any phone anywhere and get your messages played back as many times as you like. You can set up a special code so only you can play back the messages. You can, calling from outside, change the outgoing message, and even make sure no one is robbing your apartment by monitoring the room sounds—all from an outside phone in another part of the city or, by long distance, from anywhere in the world.

The major feature you need to look for, though, is the ability to call from outside and retrieve your messages. All too often, an agent will call at noon wanting you to be at an audition at one o'clock that same day. You can't afford either the time or the expense of constantly going home to check your machine for messages.

The alternative to an answering machine is an answering service. There are two kinds of answering services: The traditional service where the caller leaves a message by calling the service's number, and what are known as "pick-up" services, because they literally pick up calls that come in to your number while you are out. While pick-up services are great for doctors, dentists, and lawyers, the consensus is that performers are better off with the more traditional answering services. Probably the most persuasive reason to choose a regular answering service is that agents want to work as efficiently as possible. If you use one of the more popular theatrical answering services, the agent only has to make a single call to leave messages for a dozen or more performers who use that service. Although he may not go to the trouble of calling your home number, the agent *is* likely to include your name in his message list if he's calling a service for a number of other people. Another reason for preferring a traditional answering service, provided you have carefully chosen a "theatrical" service, is the emotional security of knowing your service employs people who are attuned to the importance of career opportunities. A service that specializes in answering the phones of real estate agents will not be as aware of the importance of an agent's call as one that specializes in theatrical performers. It is not unknown for an answering service employee, realizing the importance of a particular message, to call all over town to find their client and give him what they feel is an important communication. That's precisely what my New York service, Greenroom, did for me on one occasion. Just from an emotional viewpoint, it feels quite nice to hear someone from your service tell you with genuine enthusiasm, "Hey! You got a booking. Congratulations!"

Often, in smaller markets, there are no services that specialize in theatrical accounts. In such cases, you should probably be content with a good quality machine. In larger markets—certainly in New York—you should seriously consider one of the number of good theatrical answering services.

Some people work both sides of the street; they own an answering machine and still use a service. Aside from the initial investment for the machine, it doesn't cost any more for such redundancy, and it can be an excellent insurance policy when you consider that a single missed telephone call can potentially be worth thousands of dollars.

Make Friends and Learn Names

There is a saying to the effect that you can never have too many friends and one enemy is one too many. Good advice! Not only should you make an effort to become friendly with agents and casting directors, but also make an effort to ingratiate yourself to those who fall into the category of support personnel. Engineers, secretaries, receptionists, and switchboard operators all can, at the very least, make your professional life a little smoother, and at best, can make it a little more lucrative. Some engineers keep their own private file of demo tapes or samples of work done in their studio. Occasionally an engineer is asked by a producer for casting suggestions. Receptionists in casting departments have been known to suggest to a performer that, in addition to the spot he's there to audition for, he might want to wander down the hall where another audition is being held. The receptionist didn't have any obligation to share that information, and if the performer had, in the past, acted rudely or haughtily, the subject would simply never have come up, and he'd never know what he'd missed.

Unions

There are two unions with jurisdiction over the work of voice-over performers: the American Federation of Television and Radio Artists (AFTRA), and the Screen Actors Guild (SAG). Both unions date to before the days of television when AFTRA was known as the American Federation of Radio Artists. In those days, it was a simple matter to determine which kind of work belonged to which union. Work in films was regulated by contracts negotiated by SAG, and to this day, most members of SAG live in California, since that is where most films are still made. Radio stations cropped up all across the country and AFTRA regulated the contracts, working conditions, and rates of radio performers. So there are AFTRA locals in most major markets, although the largest locals are in New York and Los Angeles.

When television came along, it seemed only natural that AFTRA assume jurisdiction because most people, at first, thought of TV as nothing more than radio with pictures. After a while, though, some programs began to be produced on film and SAG exercised its right to control any program or commercial on film. The next development was videotape. Since AFTRA had long controlled radio programs that were recorded on audiotape, they exerted their jurisdiction over videotape as well. And that's the way it goes to this day: filmed spots come under SAG and videotaped spots under AFTRA.

Today, both unions work together in negotiating contracts for pay scales and work rules for commercial performers, both on-camera and voice-overs. Every time union elections roll around, candidates for the various offices promise to work for the merger of the two unions, but such talk has been going on for years and few members of either union hold any realistic hope of it actually happening in the near future. Meanwhile, the union you join first becomes your "parent union" and you pay full initiation fees and dues to that union. The other gives you credit for what you pay your parent union and only requires that you pay partial dues and initiation fees.

AFTRA is what's known as an open union. Anybody can walk into an AFTRA office, pay the initiation fee and the current dues, and presto! She's a member. SAG, however, won't let you join unless you can prove you have been hired to work in a film. There is one exception: if you are an AFTRA member who has worked as a principle (you had a starring part) or had at least five or more lines to speak in a spot under AFTRA's jurisdiction, SAG will consider you to be serious about your career as a commercial performer and let you join them as well. Otherwise, SAG's attitude is that you might very well have joined AFTRA simply as a way to sneak into SAG. And, since the initiation fees for AFTRA are lower than for SAG, that very thought has been known to cross some people's minds.

Fortunately for newcomers to the business, you don't have to be a member of any union to get your first job. Each union allows you one "freebie" before you have to join. So why spend the money sooner than you have to? Wait until you get your first job. With that under your belt, you can join the union with the appropriate jurisdiction, which will be your parent union. You still won't need to join the other performers' union until after you've done one spot under that second union's area.

The following information about membership in the Screen Actors Guild was provided by SAG's New York branch:

1. If the applicant is NOT a member of an affiliated Guild, he or she must present a letter from a SAG signatory motion picture producer or his representative, or from a film television or commercial company, stating that the applicant is wanted for a principal role or speaking part in a specific film not more than two weeks prior to the beginning of filming.

2. If the applicant is a currently paid-up member in good standing of an affiliated Guild (Equity, AFTRA, AGMA, AGVA, etc.) for a period of at least

one year or longer and has worked as a principal performer or the equivalent thereof in that jurisdiction at least once.

OR:

If the applicant has not been a member of an affiliated Guild for a minimum period of one year, BUT has a definite commitment for a principal or speaking role in a motion picture, filmed commercial or filmed television show, he or she will be accepted for membership into the Screen Actors Guild, not more than two weeks prior to the beginning of the filming.

The joining fee is determined at the time of application to Screen Actors Guild and is based on the amount of initiation fee paid to the affiliated Guild.

3. If the applicant has proof of employment as a principal or speaking role by a SAG signatory motion picture production company or film television or commercial company which states the applicant's name and social security number, the signatory company's name, the name of the production or the commercial (the product), the salary paid (in dollar amount form), and the specific date(s) worked, he or she will be accepted for membership. Such proof of employment may be in the form of a signed contract, or a letter from the company provided it states all the necessary information listed in this paragraph. (Original or carbon copies, not Xerox copies, are accepted.) Employment in student, experimental, university or non-signatory films does not constitute eligibility for Screen Actors Guild membership.

The joining fee is determined at the time of application to Screen Actors Guild by the method stated in paragraph 1 or 2 above.

First job as a principal denotes which Guild is parent and that union is to receive full initiation fee and dues.

The following information was provided by the national office of AFTRA in New York:

The American Federation of Television and Radio Artists is a nationwide union of over 50,000 members and is part of the Associated Actors and Artists of America (AFL-CIO). AFTRA is related in this way to the other performer unions: Actors Equity Association, American Guild of Musical Artists, American Guild of Variety Artists, Screen Actors Guild.

AFTRA is currently composed of 38 Locals throughout the United States, with National headquarters at 1350 Avenue of the Americas, New York, New York 10019. As an open union, AFTRA accepts all those who apply for membership. Initiation fees for membership are based upon income in the fields of radio, television, non-broadcasting materials, transcriptions, video-taped commercial recordings, cassettes and phonograph recordings. AFTRA is governed by its members. The members of each Local elect a Local Board of Directors and also representatives to the National Board of Directors. All Board members and officers, both Local and National, serve without remuneration. The policies and programs determined by the elected boards are administered by paid Executive Secretaries. The head administrator in AFTRA is the National Executive Secretary.

The National Board meets in regional sections: New York, Chicago and Los Angeles to transact matters of policy and operation. Locals boards meet on a regular basis and membership meetings take place in the various Locals. AFTRA holds an annual National Convention to further the aims of its members.

All persons in the fields of radio, television, non-broadcast materials, cassette and phonograph records who sing, speak, act, announce, demonstrate, play, dance, create sound effects or are performers within the fields of news, sports, weather, etc., are eligible for membership in AFTRA. This includes any person who performs as an actress, actor, singer, dancer, announcer, newscaster, narrator, lecturer, sound effects, commentator, analyst, master of ceremonies, artist, demonstrator, moderator, specialist, quiz master, disc jockey, sportscaster, specialty act, puppeteer, walk-on or extra.

In some stations, at the request of the personnel concerned, AFTRA membership is open to continuity, production, floor-people, editors and news writers, and other production or programming personnel. AFTRA is a labor organization and part of the AFL-CIO. The main and driving purpose is the protection of its members and all performers. This protection is afforded through organization, negotiation, grievance and arbitration procedures and the collective bargaining process.

AFTRA does not provide an employment service, but can provide information on rates, terms and conditions of employment throughout the country.

Advertising Agencies

Somewhere around a hundred years or so ago the American institution of the advertising agency came into being. It all started with a number of advertising salesmen working for various magazines. These men usually worked on a commission-only basis, so it was to their advantage to develop good relationships with the businesses to which they sold the ads. If salesman A sold advertising space for *Atlantic,* he would do anything to prevent his client's precious advertising dollars from going to any magazine but *Atlantic.* The salesman would even help his client write the copy; anything to keep the account happy. Some of these salesmen developed such a rapport with their clients that the clients wouldn't even talk to a salesman from another magazine. But the clients occasionally worried that, perhaps, they were missing a bit of advertising effectiveness by only putting their ads in one magazine. So salesman A went to *Harper's Magazine* and suggested he might be able to persuade his client, B, to put some of the money he usually spent with *Atlantic* into *Harper's—if Harper's* would pay him a commission. They agreed, the client was happy and salesman A didn't lose any commission; he just collected half of it from one magazine and half from another.

The next step in the process was for client B to see such good results from his advertising that he decided to increase his ad budget and place ads in a third magazine. Since salesman A seemed to have been the person who engineered all this success, his advice was again sought, and again, he scurried off to another magazine—let's say *The Saturday Evening Post.* Their salesman hadn't even been able to get in the door at client B's, so they agreed to give salesman A a commission if he could get them any of B's business.

Meanwhile, the whole arrangement was working so well for him that salesman A decided to try the same scheme with several other clients. His success inspired other magazine salesmen to do likewise, and soon the salesmen weren't really working for the magazines at all, they were working for their clients. But the magazines were still the ones who paid them. Their work got so voluminous the salesmen had to hire other salesmen as well as artists and copywriters to handle their clients' advertising. No longer were they magazine-space salesmen. They had transmogrified themselves into advertising agencies.

Today, advertising agencies work much the same way, in that the agencies work as the agents of their clients, and yet are paid by the media from whom they buy the advertising. There are minor variations and occasional cases of other financial arrangements, but by and large, that's how it operates. Perhaps a hundred years from now, the industry may operate differently; there are those in the business who see signs of such change, but we're more concerned with the here and now.

We've already talked about copywriters, producers, and casting directors. The other Important Person you will encounter from an advertising agency is the Account Executive. Account executives act as the liaison between agency and client, and therefore are the modern counterparts of the original nineteenth century magazine salesmen who started the whole thing. In smaller agencies, an account executive may handle the advertising accounts for several clients. In larger shops, each account executive is assigned to an individual account. And in major agencies, an account executive may be assigned to only one of a client's products, or even to only one campaign or aspect of a campaign.

Nonetheless, the account executive is an important person within the agency, she represents the client, and has a lot of say in routine, day-to-day matters. Although you will rarely see the account executive at an audition, she may be there for a callback and is almost always present at the final recording session. Be polite and friendly. Make a good impression not only with your work, but personally as well. It will be to your advantage the next time your name comes up for consideration as a potential voice-over.

Dealing with Rejection

Unless you have superhuman emotional stability, one of the hardest things you'll ever do is to break into a highly competitive field like voice-overs. Because of the intense competition, nobody has any reason to give you the slightest benefit of the doubt.

Even if you are able to compete on an equal footing, the numerical odds dictate that you will be rejected far more often than you are accepted. A glance at an audition sign-in sheet will show literally dozens of people auditioning for the same job. Since only one person can get each job, it follows that you will have to endure dozens of rejections for each job you get.

The most important thing to remember, in dealing with rejection, is that not getting a particular spot is no reflection either on you as a person or on your talent and ability. All it means is you were not exactly what they were looking for in this particular instance. You might not have been precisely right for this spot, but that doesn't have anything to do with your talent and ability or your worth as a person.

Another point to keep in mind is the element of luck. You may have, unknown to you, been up against the copywriter's nephew. Or, the way you wear your hair and its color may unconsciously remind the producer of the schoolyard bully who used to beat him up in the sixth grade. Who knows why we find ourselves taking an instant dislike to another person? But it does happen, and there's nothing we can do about it. So chalk it up to the luck of the draw and move on, secure in the knowledge that even the greatest men of history had their enemies.

It is vital, though, that you don't let constant rejection turn you into a sad sack. Cheerfulness begets cheerfulness and gloom inspires gloom. So even if it's one of your "down" days, make a conscious effort to appear "up." Purposely put a smile on your face. When you notice your gait is a little slow, force yourself to walk at a little more sprightly pace, and literally, keep your chin up; keep concentrating on objects above your eye level and refuse to look at the ground. Remember, when you're asked "How are you?" it's only a rhetorical question; they really don't want a recitation of your problems and ills. So make your one and only reply in all circumstances "Great! Just great, thanks!" No matter how bad you feel, no matter how dismal the day has been, always act as though you're truly glad to be alive.

Doing It for Real

I – At Last . . . an Audition!

The Call

It all begins with a phone call from an agent. He'll ask if you can make an audition this afternoon at 1:30. You, of course, say "yes," and he tells you where. He knows you are just getting started, so if it is an obscure agency or casting service, it's OK to ask him where the place is located—at least for a little while. But if you are acting even halfway professionally you'll quickly learn where the major agencies are so you don't have to ask.

Keep a copy of the *Ross Report* and get a publication called *Flashmaps Instant Guide to New York*. It has street maps of all Manhattan neighborhoods and an address-finder for midtown. The *Ross Report* will give you the agency's address and the *Flashmap* will help you figure out how to get there. Every major city will have similar publications.

The agent will also tell you what product you will be auditioning for, and usually, what kind of sound they're looking for. "They're looking for someone who sounds like a college professor" or "they want an 'Orson Wells' sound" or "the spot calls for a very authoritative 'voice of God' sound."

Most of the time, that's the way it goes. You're told where and when to show up. But if there's a choice of times, you can give yourself an advantage over some of the others who are auditioning. An audition, in a way, is a kind of job interview, and industrial psychologists have done a lot of research on interviewing techniques. One of the things they have discovered is that there is an optimum timeframe—a "window," if you will—during which your chances of being chosen are greatest. The most opportune time for you to audition is the period when the interviewer (in this case, the casting director and/or producer) is most likely to make a decision.

However long the period of time during which the auditions are being held—it's usually between two and three hours— the producer will spend the first quarter to third of the audition period getting ideas, figuring out what he wants and doesn't want. By the time he's ready to decide, he may not even remember the first few who auditioned. Eventually, he starts to pay serious attention to the people auditioning, and by the final third to quarter of the time allotted for auditioning voice-over talent, he's becoming aware that he's running out of time and had better start making some at least tentative choices. By the time the last few people audition, he may have already made his decision.

So, if you have any say in the matter, arrange to arrive somewhat after the midway point in the audition period. That way, you'll be fresh in the producer's mind when he makes his final choice. All other things being equal, it will give you an edge against your competition. Simply ask your agent, when he calls, what hours they will be holding the auditions. When he tells you, ask for the time you want. If it's possible, you'll get it. If it can't be arranged, no harm has been done, and you at least tried.

There's another way to give yourself an extra edge. Unions require casting directors to get you auditioned and out of there within one hour. Otherwise, they have to pay you for your time. So they are very conscientious about auditioning you shortly after you arrive. The usual amount of time between your arrival and the time you are called is about ten minutes. To make sure they don't accidentally keep you waiting too long, casting departments require you to sign in with your name, your agent, usually your social security number, the time you were scheduled for your audition, the time you actually arrived and the time you left. To give yourself a little extra preparation time, get there at least five minutes early, but sign in at the time you were actually scheduled. You have substantially increased the time you have to study and work on your interpretation of the copy. Voice-over professionals have been using this little trick for years and nobody has called them on it yet. Incidentally, should the casting director call you when you've really only been there two or three minutes, it is perfectly acceptable and legitimate for you to say something to the effect of "Gee, I just got here and I really haven't had a chance to look over the copy yet. Could you please take someone else now, and I'll be ready next."

At the reception desk of the casting department, there will always be a stack of photocopies of the script to be used in the audition. It usually will be right beside the sign-in sheet. If you don't see any scripts, ask for one. You have a right to be able to prepare yourself. When you get your copy of the script, go through the same steps you would for any copy: analyze it, mark it—remember, pencil only—and then practice. Practice aloud, or at least move your lips. If you feel self-conscious about practicing in front of others, walk over to a remote corner of the room or down the hall a few paces. And don't be surprised if you find someone else down there doing exactly what you're doing. Incidentally, since pencil sharpeners aren't necessarily part of casting department equipment, always have at least *two* well-sharpened pencils with you.

You'll hear a lot of interesting conversation in the waiting area and you'll be tempted to join in. Don't! Use the little time you have to work on the copy. After you've done *your* audition, you can come back and chat all you want on the other person's preparation time.

Some of the larger agencies have elaborate recording studios. Some smaller ones have no studio at all; your audition will be made on an old, broken-down home recorder. Regardless of the size of the agency, no matter what kind of equipment you use, the audition is important for you, so do your very best. Give them a strong interpretation; pull out all the stops. They can always bring you down a little, but if your first interpretation is a weak one, they may think that's all you are capable of and the audition will be over right there.

When your audition is indeed over, be pleasant. Thank everyone. Leave them with a good impression, because there's always tomorrow's audition to think of.

After the Audition

There's an old saying; "the job's not finished until you do the paperwork." Since you're approaching your voice-over career as a business, you have to take care of the business part of it immediately after each audition. Don't wait, and don't put it off until tomorrow. As soon as you come in and take off your coat, sit down and send out your post cards. One to the agent for sending you up for the job and one to the casting director saying "thanks" for the opportunity to read. Any little personal note you can add to help him remember you is good. Refer to your conversation. Say how you hope his tennis elbow is better soon or tell him again how sorry you were to hear that his pet parrot died. Anything that will make him remember you . . . fondly. Don't be cute. And above all, don't make a pitch for the job you auditioned for. By the time your card reaches him, the decision will have already been made.

The final card is one you fill out for yourself so that four or five months from now you'll be able to remember who you au-

ditioned for, where, and who told you what. If you already have a
file card or computer entry on this particular casting agent, just
update it. If you don't have an entry on him, make one. The next
time you audition for that person, you'll be able to look him up
and recall all the important details of your previous encounters. It
will flatter him to think you remember him so well. You'll be glad
that your records were kept so carefully and in such detail.

You can sit by the phone if you like, but it's a needless
form of self-torture. Whatever you do, resist the temptation to call
your agent or, even worse, the casting director. If there's any good
news, your *agent* will call *you*. It might be in an hour or two. More
likely, it will be in a day or two; possibly even a week or two.

If and when the call does come, remain calm. Get all the
details and write them down. Read them back to your agent to
make sure you have them all down correctly. Once you hang up
the phone, you can let out a big whoop for joy. Just maintain your
dignity until then.

11 – The Recording Session

The night before the big day, get lots of sleep. Set two alarms to
be sure you don't oversleep. Get up in plenty of time to leisurely
shower and dress and eat a light but nourishing breakfast. Allow
yourself enough time for traffic jams and still plan to get to the recording at least fifteen minutes early. And don't forget *two* sharp-
ened pencils.

In Chapter 1, when we talked about recording studios,
we failed to mention the one piece of equipment you will find in
every recording studio in the United States; a coffee machine.
Find the machine and have a cup. Then get a copy of the script
and review it carefully. Chances are it has been revised since you
last saw it. If you're lucky, they've decided by now to do more
than one version of the spot, or even several different spots. It

may have been weeks since you auditioned, so go through the whole routine again: analysis, interpretation, marking.

If you have any questions—about pronunciation, your cue, anything at all—don't be afraid to ask. The producer is there, and probably the copywriter as well. Maybe the account executive, too. Even the client. And, of course, the engineer. They're all there for one thing: to make you sound as good as you possibly can. So if you need anything, just ask.

The actual recording process isn't too much different from what you did at the audition. You do a take. The producer makes some adjustments. You do another take. More suggestions from the producer. And so on and so on.

Cues

When do you start to talk? It depends on the kind of spot you're doing. If it's a simple audio spot, the engineer will do the slate and you're free to take a deep breath and start at will. If, however, you're working on a television spot, you may need to get your cue from the video. Let's say, for example, your cue to talk is when the picture cuts to a close-up of the detergent box. You will probably have seen a storyboard and they will almost always run the video portion for you a few times so that you can become familiar with it. From the storyboard, and watching the video, you have noticed that the last thing we see before the close-up of the box is a lady picking up a folded bath towel. You make note of this on the script so that when you see her hand start to reach for the towel, you can take a deep breath, and the second the close-up appears, you are starting to talk. Note that everyone instinctively takes a breath before they begin to speak. If you wait for your cue before you take that breath, you will consistently be late with your cue. So always anticipate your cue, and have your lungs filled with air before the cue arrives.

Sometimes your cue is an audio cue. When you hear the line "I'm having corn flakes." you say "Hope you're hungry.

You'll have to eat six bowls to match the vitamins in Total." Then you wait until you hear "I'm eating shredded wheat" at which point you come back with "you're eating twelve bowls full!" What you hear through the headphones will cue you to speak. Again, make sure you anticipate the cue, take your breath beforehand and are ready to speak the moment you hear your cue.

There are two other common ways of getting cues. If the spot is shot on film, the movie screen you are watching will have a footage counter displayed, usually directly below the screen. If the spot is on video tape, you'll have a monitor to watch and a running time reference will be superimposed over either the top or bottom of the screen. Either way, just watch the counter. As your magic number approaches, take your breath and when the number hits the screen, you start talking.

The dean of voice-over performers, the late Alexander Scourby,was said to have refused to ever do more than three takes of a spot. Frank Sinatra, when making films and phonograph records, is said to never have done more than one take. These are two very rare exceptions to what, otherwise, is an almost universal rule: It is rare, if ever, that you will get a perfect take on the first try. Multiple takes are the rule, not the exception. Sometimes it takes four or five takes. Sometimes it takes ten or fifteen. Sometimes it takes twenty or thirty. Sometimes you'll blow a word or two. Don't let it bother you. No matter how experienced the professional, she still will occasionally bobble a word now and then. It's part of the condition known as being human. The thing that marks the professional from the amateur is that while the amateur gets flustered, turns red in the face and apologizes profusely, the professional realizes it's just one of those things and says calmly, "I'm sorry. Let's try another take."

Your mistakes are only a minor reason for multiple takes. More often, another take is needed when the producer has gotten an inspiration and wants you to try yet another interpretation. Maybe she wants you to try a little chuckle on the word "friendliest." Or maybe she's decided she wants some irony in your voice when you mention the competitor's product. Whatever she wants, do your very best to give it to her; that's what you're being paid to do. Work with her until, by your collaborative efforts, you come up with a take that you are both delighted with.

Pick-Ups

Sometimes you will get all the way through a spot superbly—perfectly, even—and blow the next to last line. In such cases, it is frequently the practice to do what is called a *pick-up*. Instead of doing the entire spot over again from the top, you go back to a point about two or three sentences before the spot you bobbled and begin from there. The engineer will then physically or electronically edit the new ending onto the original recording.

      This same term, pick-up, is sometimes used to describe what are also called tags or tag-lines. These occur when there are a number of spots that are identical except for the last line, which differs depending on time or location. In such cases, you record the body of the spot once. Then you record "Available at Macy's. (pause) Available at Bloomingdales. (pause) Available at Woodward & Lothrup." Another common example: "Monday on HBO. Tuesday on HBO. Wednesday on HBO . . . Tomorrow on HBO. Today on HBO. Tonight on HBO." The key to such pick-ups is to do them all the same. Unlike listings where you strive to read each item differently, with pick-ups you should make them as identical as possible in tone, energy level, and inflection.

Don't Get Paranoid

Because you are viewed as the hired hand and are expected to be able to do any kind of delivery and interpretation they want upon demand, the producer, copywriter and others in the control room tend to ignore you when they get into discussions about creative matters. You finish a take and you are asked to "stand by" for a moment. Maybe you aren't told anything at all. You just finish the take and you stand there. You haven't the slightest idea what is going on except for what you see through the soundproof window, which is a group of people engaged in a heated conversation.

Your natural reaction to these circumstances, especially if you're new to the business, is to think "Ohmygawd! They're talking about *me*. They don't like my voice. They think I can't do it right. They're sorry they hired me. They want to get somebody else to do the spot."

Remember: if they didn't like your voice and your style they wouldn't have hired you to begin with. Watching those conferences behind the glass can be frustrating and even intimidating. But they invariably turn out to be over whether they should change the word "delicious" to "luscious"—not about you.

Beware of paranoia!

Dubs for Your Reel

Whenever you finish doing a spot, always ask politely if you can have a dub for your demo reel. The person to ask is the engineer. If he has any reservations, he may ask you to clear it with the producer. You will almost always get an OK. Sometimes, though, they may want to keep the script secret until after the spot goes on the air. Make it clear that you will be more than happy to come back to the studio after the spot has begun airing to pick up your dub.

Always, as a courtesy, offer to pay for the dub. You'll rarely have to do it; they have so many dubs to make for the agency that making one more is no big deal. But by doing so, they are doing you a favor, and you should acknowledge that fact by making the offer to pay. One voice-over veteran who follows this form has only once in his entire career actually been charged for the dub.

What do you do with these dubs? Well, once you have three or four of them, you take them to a recording studio and update your demo reel. Take out the ones you like the least or those that are the oldest and put in the new ones or the ones you like better. Eventually, you should reach the point where you are sending out a brand new demo reel every year or so. Sure, it's expensive. But when you're working so much that you have the material to do a new tape every year, the cost is a drop in the bucket compared to the potential business it can generate for you.

Son of Paperwork

Before you leave the recording session, you'll have to fill out releases giving them the right to use your voice. They are standard forms, and are kept by the agency's legal department and filed with AFTRA or SAG as well.

The paperwork continues when you get home. Send those postcards again. Thank everyone involved in this job, tell everybody else on your mailing list about what you've just done, and alert them to listen for it on the air.

In a few weeks, you get to do the best paperwork of all. You open the envelope, remove the check, endorse it, and deposit it in your bank account.

May it happen many, many, many times for you!

Suggested Reading

To better understand the advertising industry and the way commercials are made:

Arlen, Michael J. *Thirty Seconds*. Penguin Books, 1980.

Della Femina, Jerry. *From Those Wonderful Folks Who Gave You Pearl Harbor*. Pocket Books, 1970.

Ogilvy, David. *Confessions of an Advertising Man*. Ballantine Books, 1964.

Packard, Vance. *The Hidden Persuaders*. Washington Square Press, 1957, 1980.

Schwartz, Tony. *Media: The Second God*. Random House, 1981.

Schwartz, Tony. *The Responsive Chord*. Anchor Press, 1973.

Shanks, Bob. *The Cool Fire*. Vintage Books, 1977.

For an insight into the business of acting—both theatrical and commercial:

Fridel, Squire. *Acting In Television Commercials*. Harmony Books, 1980.

Hayes, Vangie. *How To Get Into Commercials*. Harper & Row, 1983.

Peacock, James. *How To Audition for Television Commercials and Get Them*. Contemporary Books, 1982.

Shurtleff, Michael. *Audition*. Walker & Co., 1978.

Weist, Dwight and Robert Barron. *On Camera*. Walker & Co., 1982.

A good source of copy:

One Club, The. *Art Director's Annual*. 1980, et al.

Sample
Copy

Merrill Lynch

Today, the landscape of investment opportunity spreads far and wide,
but there is one place they grow in all varieties to suit every kind of
investor. At Merrill Lynch we've brought together a profusion of financial
services to nurture all kinds of investment needs, and it is the skill
and care with which we tend them that makes us what we are. Merrill Lynch.
A breed apart.

SAMSONITE LUGGAGE

For most luggage, travel can become a real torture test. For
soft sided luggage to survive, it must be as durable, as it
is lightweight. To survive it must be rugged. In the way
it's designed, the way it's made. That's why more people
travel with Samsonite. Because, when you survive the trip,
so should your luggage. Samsonite, the survivor.

SPRINGHOUSE WATER 986
ONE MINUTE (Label) #2
for use anytime
1/12/81

PLAY ET FOLLOWED BY:

ANNCR: Here's one of the reasons the people at Springhouse say "we couldn't
make Springhouse any better, 'cause we didn't make it. Next time
you're at the supermarket or deli, take a close look at the label on a
bottle of Springhouse Truly Natural Spring Water. You'll see an
ingredient list that names the minerals nature puts in Springhouse.
All water contains a selection of minerals in one form or another. But
Springhouse is the bottled water that tells you exactly what you get—
truly natural, completely unprocessed spring water with a delicate
balance of minerals. Springhouse takes pride in that. So they
tell you—right on the label.

CLIENT THE HOOVER	#9995-003-	DATE AND TIME	FEBRUARY
COMPANY	804	TO BE USED	11-13, 198-
PROGRAM GIMBELS/			
NEW YORK		LENGTH OF	
STATION WNBC & WABC		COMMERCIAL	:30

ANNCR:
LIVE

YOU'RE INVITED TO GIMBELS BIGGEST HOOVER SALE EVER! COME SAVE 15 TO 50% ON EVERY HOOVER CLEANER IN STOCK...THERE ARE BARGAINS GALORE!! GET HOOVER'S POPULAR UPRIGHT FOR ONLY $59.99...YOU SAVE 50 PER-CENT!! OR SAVE 37% ON HOOVER'S CELEBRITY CANISTER WITH ATTACHMENTS...JUST $49.99 AT GIMBELS. AND HOOVER'S QUIK-BROOM IS SALE PRICED AT $29.99...SAVE 33%!! EVEN HOOVER BAGS ARE HALF-PRICE! SO SAVE 15 TO 50 PERCENT NOW DURING GIMBELS BIGGEST HOOVER SALE EVER!

KONI—TV Script :30   2/28/8-

One shock absorber is so superior it has been used by every World
Champion for the past 13 years.
KONI...

KONI—So superior they're standard
          on every Ferrari...
          on every Aston Martin...
          on the exciting new Mustang SVO.

KONI—The ultimate performance shock.
          Adjustable for wear.
          Less body lean...
          More stability,
          Crisper handling.
          Put the world's finest
          performance shocks on your car.

KONI—Proven Superior.

HOME PRIDE

WHEN TENDER YOUNG TURKEY IS BASTED WITH BUTTER, YOU
CAN PRACTICALLY TASTE IT WITH YOUR EYES. AND STRUDEL
LAYERED WITH BUTTER. . . YOU CAN ALMOST SEE HOW GOOD IT'S
GOING TO TASTE. IT'S THE SAME WITH HOME PRIDE BUTTER TOP WHEAT
. . .
BAKED WITH BUTTER, BRAN AND HONEY. IT LOOKS AND TASTES
LIKE REAL WHEAT BREAD SHOULD, BECAUSE WE SPLIT THE TOP,
ADD BUTTER AND LET IT BAKE RIGHT IN.
HOME PRIDE BUTTER TOP. . . WHEAT AND WHITE. YOU CAN
PRACTICALLY TASTE IT WITH YOUR EYES.

**THE NEW
SCHOOL (:30)**

TIME: _____

DATE: _____

Make 1984 your best year ever! Consider attending The New School,
in Greenwich Village, and learn new skills, explore new ideas,
meet new people, or prepare for a new career. Do it *all* at The
New School, America's First University for Adults, where there are
more than 2,000 courses to choose from . There's a whole new world
to explore in 1984, and taking the first step couldn't be easier.
Call right now for your free New School catalog. 245-3900. Be
part of the New Year at the New School! Call 245-3900.

11/30/8-

TELEVISION SPOT: FIAT

Last year was a rotten year for cars
Volkswagen sales were down

Vega down

Toyota down

        Gremlin down

Datsun down

Capri, Opel Mazda down

Of these leading small cars last year . . . only 1 was up

Fiat

It was our best year ever

TELEVISION SPOT
TRI-STATE CHEVROLET

LET'S TALK ABOUT A COUPLE OF NUMBER ONES. YOU AND YOUR TRI-STATE CHEVROLET DEALER. YOU, BECAUSE YOU'RE LOOKING OUT FOR NUMBER ONE AND WANT A REAL VALUE ON A QUALITY NEW CAR. YOUR TRI-STATE CHEVY DEALER BECAUSE HE'S GOT THE NUMBER ONE SELLING CAR IN AMERICA—THE CHEVY CAVALIER. AS A MATTER OF FACT, YOUR TRI-STATE CHEVY DEALER HAD SIX DIFFERENT CAVALIER MODELS, BASE STICKER PRICED UNDER $7,000. SO LOOK OUT FOR NUMBER ONE. LOOK FOR THE NUMBER ONE SELLING CAVALIER. LOOK TO YOUR TRI-STATE CHEVY DEALER.

Pilot Life
:30 TV
"Two Kinds"

VIDEO   **AUDIO**

(Music under throughout)

VO: There are two kinds of people.
One only buys a life insurance
policy.
The other gets a complete financial
plan from a professional Pilot Life
representative.
As they mature, so do their investments.
But one man's money grows more...
Thanks to the Pilot Life representative's
knowledge of business insurance,
universal life, IRA's and mutual funds.
Which proves there are two kinds of
people...
The haves...had the have-mores.
Pilot Life...
We never forget behind every policy
is a person.

DELTA #5796Y

TIME: _____

DATE: _____

Now, Delta Air Lines puts new freedom into freedom fares to
Florida. . . new freedom that makes it easier for you to save
money on round-trips to Miami, Ft. Lauderdale, Tampa/St. Pete
and other cities. Delta freedom fares give you 20-to-25 per cent
off regular day tourist fares. And now you can get your Delta
reservation and buy your ticket just one week before you leave.
You can fly back as soon as the first Monday after you leave
New York, or you can stay until mid-December. That means you
can go for a weekend trip, or a week-long visit, or even longer.
No other airline makes it easier for you. And no other airline
has a lower fare. Starting September 15th, it's just 157 dollars,
round-trip, to Miami or Ft. Lauderdale on night coach flights. . .
only 168 on daytime round-trips. And Delta has over a dozen
nonstops every day to Miami/Ft. Lauderdale. For reservations,
and for full details about the new freedom in freedom fares,
call Delta Air Lines or see your travel agent. Delta is ready
when you are.

GTE SYMPHONY HALL
(:55)
Gro-Lux GTC-R 45053
(Rev. 1)
Code #GNCP-R-4106)

TIME: _____

DATE: _____

How does your garden grow? Your indoor garden, that is. Today, believe it or not, you can grow just about anything indoors as well as out. Not just African violets...but also geraniums, azaleas, ferns, gloxinias...even orchids. The secret is Gro-Lux...a special fluorescent lamp from GTE Sylvania. Gro-Lux lamps bathe your plants in light that stimulates their growth, so they flourish even in dark corners that never see a ray of sunshine. Simply illuminate your plants for roughly the number of hours they'd ordinarily have in the climate that suits them best—northern, tropical, desert...anything you want! And, if you're concerned about energy, you should know that a 40-watt Gro-Lux produces more light than a 100-watt incandescent lamp...at less than half the energy. Gro-Lux lamps...another product to make your life a little nicer, from General Telephone & Electronics—a growing concern for your growing needs.

CLIENT	THE BANK OF NEW YORK	
PRODUCT	TRUST & INVESTMENT— Your Executor	DATE STATION
PROGRAM		COMMERCIAL BNYR-4613

ANNOUNCER

The person responsible for carrying out the terms of your will is your executor. But what if your executor needs an executor before you do? The bank that manages money provides a continuity no individual executor can provide. An expertise few individuals possess. Yet, it is not more expensive to have The Bank of New York as your executor or co-executor. Indeed, it may cost less. Because the bank that manages money has groups specially trained to deal with the often complex investment, tax and accounting problems. Also, the size of The Bank of New York is such that the officers can give their personal attention to your family and its problems. Yet, there is group judgment and sympathetic impartiality on questions of discretionary disbursements, such as principal invasions. The bank is always accessible. Works in complete confidence. Is understanding...Is flexible...Is financially responsible and accountable...Is experienced...In every way, endeavors to do for your family what you would do yourself. The Bank of New York. The bank that has never confused bigness with excellence.

Index